Fishing Mapbook

Backroad Mapbooks

Kawarthas Ontario

Table of Contents

www.backroadmapbooks.com

Fishing Mapbooks

DIRECTORS
Russell Mussio
Wesley Mussio
Penny Stainton-Mussio

ASSOCIATE DIRECTOR
Jason Marleau

VICE PRESIDENT
Chris Taylor

COVER DESIGN & LAYOUT
Farnaz Faghihi

COVER PHOTO
Jason Marleau

CREATIVE CONTENT
Russell Mussio
Wesley Mussio

PRODUCTION MANAGER
Brett Firth

PRODUCTION
Andrew Allen
Farnaz Faghihi
Colin Holdener
Dale Tober

SALES / MARKETING
Jason Marleau
Chris Taylor

WRITER
Jason Marleau

National Library of Canada Cataloguing in Publication Data

Marleau, Jason, 1972-
Kawarthas, Ontario, fishing mapbook [cartographic material] / Jason
Marleau. -- 2nd ed.

Previously published under title: Fishing Ontario : Kawarthas.
"Ontario lakes guide".
"Backroad mapbooks".
Includes index.
ISBN 1-894556-92-5

1. Fishing--Ontario--Kawartha Lakes (Lakes)--Maps. 2. Kawartha Lakes (Ont. : Lakes)--Maps. I. Title.

G1147.K38E63M37 2006   799.1'09713'67   C2006-900344-0

Published by:

Backroad Mapbooks

5811 Beresford St
Burnaby, BC, V5J 1K1
P. (604) 438-3474   F. (604) 438-3470
E-mail: info@backroadmapbooks.com
www.backroadmapbooks.com
Copyright © 2006 Mussio Ventures Ltd.

Acknowledgement

This book could not have been compiled without the help of the Backroad Mapbooks team working for Mussio Ventures Ltd. Thank you Jason Marleau for your efforts and knowledge to pull together the research and writing. When combined with the talented team of Andrew Allen, Farnaz Faghihi, Brett Firth, Colin Holdener, Chris Taylor, and Dale Tober we were able to produce this comprehensive guidebook.

We would also like to thank Steve Coombes, Larry Bradt and the staff of the Ministry of Natural Resources for their assistance and patience in helping us track down the best lakes in the area. In addition, we would like to thank all those individuals, retailers and tourism personnel for their knowledge and expertise to help bolster the information on these lakes. A special thank you also goes to Sharon and Ron Marleau for their continued help and support of the Ontario projects.

Finally we would like to thank Allison, Devon, Jasper, Nancy, Madison and Penny Mussio for their continued support of the Backroad Mapbook Series. As our family grows, it is becoming more and more challenging to break away from it all to explore our beautiful country.

Sincerely,

Russell and Wesley Mussio

Help us Help you!

A comprehensive resource such as this **Fishing Mapbook** for Kawarthas Ontario could not be put together without a great deal of help and support. Despite our best efforts to ensure that everything is accurate, errors do occur. If you see any errors or omissions, please continue to let us know.

Please contact us at:
Mussio Ventures Ltd.
5811 Beresford St, Burnaby, B.C. V5J 1K1

Email: updates@backroadmapbooks.com

P: 604-438-3474 toll free 1-877-520-5670 F: 604-438-3470

All updates will be posted on our web site:
www.backroadmapbooks.com

Photo by - Jason Marleau

Disclaimer

The lake charts contained in this book are not intended for navigational purposes. Uncharted rocks and shoals may exist. Mussio Ventures Ltd. does not warrant that the information contained in this guide is correct. Therefore, please be careful when using this or any source to plan and carry out your outdoor recreation activity. Also note that travelling on logging roads, trails and waterways is inherently dangerous, and you may encounter poor road conditions, unexpected traffic, poor visibility, and low or no road/trail maintenance. Please use extreme caution when travelling logging roads, trails and waterways.

Please refer to the Ontario Recreational Fishing Regulations Summary for closures and restrictions. It is your responsibility to know when and where closures and restrictions apply.

Backroad Mapbooks

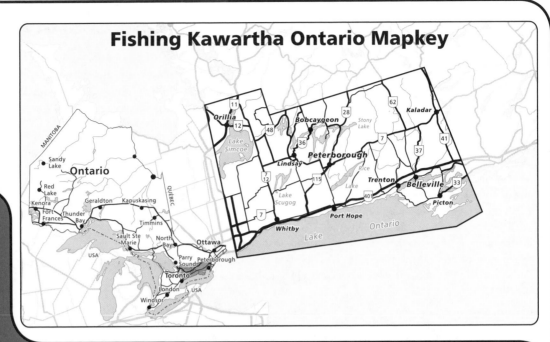

Fishing Kawartha Ontario Mapkey

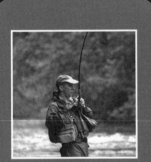

Welcome to the 2nd edition of the Kawarthas Ontario Fishing Mapbook Series. We have expanded the popular first edition to include new lakes, updated lake information and even more fishing tips to help you explore the best lakes in the Kawartha region of Ontario. The coloured depth charts combined with the valuable information on such things as access, facilities, fishing tips and stocking will allow you to choose that ideal lake for your fishing adventure. The amazing feature of this guidebook is the fact that it provides you with detailed information on where on the lake to fish. This information is invaluable to increase your success and is especially important to anglers visiting a lake for the first time.

The Kawarthas has a long heralded history as a fantastic fishing destination. The region is home to hundreds of beautiful lakes and water bodies that are comprised of mainly warm water along with a few cold water bodies located in the northern portion of the region. This unique collection of cool and warm water lakes provides an endless array of angling opportunities. Bass are the main species found in the region as largemouth bass or smallmouth bass or both are usually found in most Kawartha lakes alongside other sport fish species. However, the most popular species is walleye or pickerel, which are also found in most lakes in the area. Alternatively, larger sport fish such as the veracious muskellunge and the deep holding lake trout prefer to roam the larger water bodies.

The area covered by this book begins around the towns of Kinmount and Apsley and spans south all the way to Lake Ontario. The western border is made up of Lake Simcoe and pans eastward all the way to Belleville. The lakes in the region vary from the popular Trent-Severn Waterway chain of lakes, such as Rice Lake, to small backcountry lakes. Although these popular lakes are home to cottages and can be busy destinations during the summer months, they do offer good boat launch facilities and all the amenities you need to make a nice fishing holiday. For a more remote type setting, look for lakes in the sections between the main highways, like the areas between Highway 62 and Highway 28 or between Highway 28 and County Road 507.

The Kawarthas offers a well developed system of roads, providing easy access to most of the lakes in the region. There is also a good collection of harder to reach lakes in the region that require 4wd or are only accessible by trail or portage. For more detailed access information to all the lakes in the Kawarthas, we recommend consulting the Backroad Mapbook Series. Their Cottage Country Ontario and Eastern Ontario editions provide very detailed maps along with information on everything from camping areas to other fishing opportunities. They are the perfect companions to the Fishing Mapbook book for the Kawarthas Ontario.

The Fishing Mapbook Series is designed to show you where and how to fish any given lake. To ensure you have a successful trip, we have provided fishing tips, breakdowns of each fish species, stocking information, access and facilities as well as alternative fishing holes in the area. To compliment the writing we provide a colour depth chart for each lake as well as an overview map combined with an access map showing you where the lake is located.

No other source combines such detailed information on how and where to fish the lakes of Ontario. If you are new to the area or are looking for a new place to fish, we are certain you will find the Fishing Mapbook an excellent guide.

How to Read the Depth Charts

Knowing how to read a depth chart will definitely improve your fishing success. Depth charts are the best way to find clues to where fish are hanging out. When reading depth charts there are some general rules that can help your angling success.

When analyzing a depth chart, look for hidden islands, drop-offs and shoals. A hidden island is a relatively flat, shallow area that is slightly submerged, while being surrounded by deeper water. A drop-off is a rapid decline in the depth on the chart. A shoal is a slowly declining area of the lake, which then drops off into the depths. In larger lakes, shoals can also be characterized as shallow irregularities in the bottom of the lake, essentially, a bump in the bottom. In some lakes there may be only one or two of these significant shoal sites and often are the site of some of the best angling on the lake. Shoals often produce thicker aquatic vegetation that is home to insects and baitfish for the larger fish to feed on.

When looking for a species like lake trout, depth information can be very handy. As an example, during summer lake trout often revert to the deepest part of the lake in order to find colder water. On some lakes, there may be limited areas where lake trout will find the required depth needed for survival. With a depth chart in hand, these deep spots can be easily located.

Creek and river estuaries are always important areas to note on any lake. Fish tend to congregate near the inflows and outflows of lakes in search of increased oxygen levels and food. At times, these areas can be the hottest spot in a lake. As an example, during the fall period, walleye will often congregate near river inflows, as a part of their migration to spawning grounds.

If you read a depth chart properly, you can find very useful information. This information should allow you to improve your angling experience on the given lake or water body.

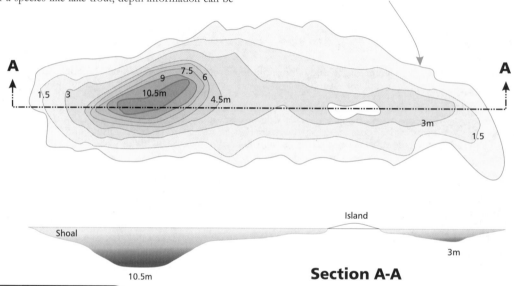

Section A-A

CAUSION:

DO NOT USE THE DEPTH CHARTS FOR NAVIGATIONAL PURPOSES.

The charts may not reflect current conditions. Uncharted hazards may exist.

The base maps for the lake charts are courtesy of the Ontario Ministry of Natural Resources.

DEPTH CHART LEGEND

GEOGRAPHIC FEATURES & ROADS

- Flooded Land
- Native Reserve
- Swamp / Marsh
- Provincial Park
- Rocks
- Sandbar
- Shoal
- Water Vegetation

- Highway
- Main Road
- Stream
- Side Road
- Old Road/Trail
- Lake

MAP & RECREATION SYMBOLS

- ⚓ Anchorage
- Boat Launch
- Lodge / Resort
- ● Community
- = Dam
- Float Plane Access
- 5 Highway, Primary
- 5A Highway, Secondary
- Highway, Trans-Canada
-)(Footbridge
- Dock/Wharf

- Hiking
- Lighthouse
- No Fishing
- P Parking
- Picnic Area
- ★ Point of Interest
- Truck Only Campground
- Trail or Water Access Campsite
- Trailer and Tent Campground
- Waterfall
- Cabins

ABBREVIATIONS

CA	Catchables
FG	Fingerling
FF	Fall Fry
YE	Yearlings
Rb	Rainbow
ha	Hectare
ac	Acre
4wd	Four Wheel Drive Vehicles
ft	Feet
m	Meters
kg	Kilogram
lbs	Pounds

Fish Species

Brook Trout

Brook trout are also known as speckled trout due to the red spots with blue halos on their sides. They are native in many streams and lakes in the Kawarthas. Brookies are often a fickle and difficult fish to catch and can sometimes be 'spooked' by even talking too loud on a lake. Inland lakes can produce brook trout to 1 kg (2.2 lbs) and sometimes larger. One of the most effective methods of angling for brookies is fly fishing. Small spoons and spinners tipped with worms can also be productive and is the recommended set up when fishing for brook trout through the ice. Due to extensive over fishing; however, most native brook trout lakes in the region must now be stocked in order to offer productive angling opportunities. The Ontario record brook trout is 6.58 kg (14.5 lbs).

Lake Trout

Lakers can grow to sizes exceeding 6 kg (13 lbs) although in smaller lakes they average about 2-3 kg (4-7 lbs). Lake trout can be found near the surface in spring when the temperature level throughout the lake is generally constant. During spring, lakers of all sizes can be caught with spinning gear virtually anywhere in the lake. As summer approaches, they retreat to colder water depths that require down rigging equipment. Spoons, spinners, or anything that imitates the lake trout's main food source, the minnow, are good choices when angling for lakers. Lake trout continue to be one of the most heavily fished species in the province and in the Kawarthas. Recent declines in lake trout stocks in Kawartha area lakes are due mostly to over harvesting by anglers; therefore, the use of catch and release fishing can go a long way in helping maintain populations. The Ontario record lake trout is 28.6 kg (63.12 lbs).

Largemouth Bass

Largemouth are widely dispersed throughout the Kawarthas, and often are found in lakes along with smallmouth bass. The warmer lakes of the region make great habitat for this warm water species. In lakes with largemouth bass, top water lures and flies can create excellent action. Plastic jigs or any minnow imitation lure or fly can also be productive. Largemouth bass are readily adaptable to warm water lakes and generally grow larger than its cousin, the smallmouth bass. The Ontario record largemouth bass is 4.7 kg (10.43 lbs).

Northern Pike

The pike is the close cousin of the muskellunge and inhabits weedy, murky waters throughout the Kawarthas. Pike can be quite aggressive at times and readily strike fast moving spoons, and spinners. In the Kawarthas they average about 1-3 kg (2-7 lbs) although can be found over 8 kg (17.6 lbs) in size, especially in the Lake Simcoe and Bay of Quinte. The main food source for this predator is other fish. Colourful spoons or flies can be very productive baits. Ontario's record northern pike is 19.11 kg (42.13 lbs).

Muskellunge

Otherwise known as 'muskie', this warm water predator feeds mainly on other fish and occasionally small mammals. Muskellunge are the largest freshwater sport fish species in Ontario and can reach over 16 kg (35 lbs) in size. The most effective method for finding these large fish is by trolling long plugs and lures in calm bays where they often cruise for food. Fall is a productive time of year. A true muskie angler releases their catch to grow larger and to be caught another day. The Ontario record muskellunge weighed 29.5 kg (65 lbs) and was caught in Blackstone Harbour of the Kawarthas.

Rainbow Trout

Rainbow are native to the Pacific Northwest and by the late 1800's had been stocked into each of the Great Lakes. Today rainbow trout have also been introduced into many inland lakes in Ontario, although spawning success is limited in these lakes. The cool waters of numerous lakes of the Kawarthas have made fine environments for stocked rainbows. It is not uncommon to find fish in the 8 kg (18 lb) range in the Great Lakes, while inland lake sizes of rainbow trout usually average 35-45 cm (14-18 in). Fly fishing can be a very productive method for inland rainbows, although small spinners and spoons also provide results. The Ontario record rainbow trout is 13.2 kg (29.12 lbs).

Smallmouth Bass

Smallmouth are found throughout the Kawarthas and are the close cousin of the largemouth bass. The smallmouth has a reputation of putting up a great fight when hooked and can be a very aggressive feeder at times. They readily strikes jigs, spinners, spoons and other fast moving lures that look like a good meal. The smallmouth can be found around structure such as shoals, islands and drop-offs. The Ontario record smallmouth bass is 4.5 kg (9.84 lbs).

Splake

Splake are sporadically stocked in various Kawartha lakes to reduce pressure on native trout lakes and to enhance angling opportunities. The species is a sterile cross between lake trout and brook trout and was developed specifically to stock lakes uninhabited by other trout species. Splake grow very rapidly similar to brook trout and to sizes similar to lake trout. Characteristic to both lake trout and brook trout, splake are most active in winter and in spring just after ice off. They will strike shiny spoons and spinners similar to lake trout and retreat to deeper water as summer approaches.

Walleye

Walleye are also known as pickerel and are perhaps the most prized sport fish in Ontario. The walleye's diet is made up of mainly baitfish, although they do take leeches and other grub like creatures. Jigs are the lure of choice either through the ice or during open water season. Walleye travel in loose schools and once you find them, you should be able to catch more than one. Jigging in set locations or trolling slowly along weed beds can entice walleye strikes. Walleye are most active during the darker times of day, hence, early morning and evening are the most productive periods. The Ontario record walleye is 10.1 kgs (22.25 lbs).

Fishing Tips & Techniques

Spincasting

The most popular angling method used in Ontario today is spincasting. Essentially, spincasting is the process of casting a line from a rod with a spinning reel. The spincasting set up is quite simple making it easy for anyone to learn how to fish and have fun at it.

Equipment

There are a number of variations of spinning type reels available on the market today, although the two main types of spin reels are the closed face reel and the open face reel.

The difference between the two reels is quite basic. The line and action of the closed face reel is encased in order to help prevent tangling of the line. The line is cast by the simple point and click of a button on the reel. This type of reel has become the reel of choice of professional and recreational anglers over the past few years and has many advantages, most notably the ease of operation. One drawback is that the access to the line on the reel is limited.

Open face reels offer the angler full access to the line on the reel and control of the cast. The angler can actually hold the line with the index finger during the cast, aiding (or perhaps hindering) in the control of the cast. An advantage of this type of reel is mainly the access to the line. More subtle flip type casts are also easier with this type of reel. One drawback of the open face reel is that it takes a little more dexterity to throw a cast and tangling can be a problem with cheaper versions.

Basically, both reels can be used in almost any situation; therefore, the type of reel you choose to use should be based on personal preference.

Spincasting Lures

At any of your local tackle shops, you will find a seemingly endless array of tackle. From the hundreds of versions of the spinner to the simple jig head and body, it can be a confusing decision. Here is a quick rundown of the lures and what they are mainly used for:

Spinners

There is a wide variety of spinners available. Countless variations and brands can produce results, including brand names such as Mepps or Blue Fox. The spinner is a versatile lure that can provide success for trout, bass and pike on occasion. The spinner is a very active lure and is usually worked quickly within about the 1-3 m (3-10 ft) depth range.

Spoons

Spoons come in a mix of sizes and colours. Spoons are more commonly used when fishing for pike and trout; however they can be productive for other species as well. For pike, the larger presentations with brighter colours, like red or yellow, are the spoons of choice. For trout, smaller silver or gold spoons can be productive and often sport shades of blue, or green. A popular brand name for trout spoons is the Little Cleo, while the Red Devil is a long heralded pike spoon.

Jigs

Jigs are made up of a weighted head and plastic body. Both the head and body come in a wide range of colours, shapes and sizes. As with any lure, the key to finding a successful, size or colour is done mainly through trial and error. Jigs work well for bass and are a favourite lure of walleye anglers. The single hook nature of the jig is also somewhat resistant, providing the ability to be worked effectively through weeds, unlike most other lures.

Crankbaits

This type of lure is essentially a piece of painted plastic shaped to wobble when reeled through the water. As with any lure, there are hundreds of different crankbaits on the market. The crankbait can be productive for a wide variety of sport fish, but most notably for, walleye, pike and bass. The main advantage of any crankbait is its unique movement ability.

Top Water Lures

Some of the most exciting fishing is done with top water lures. Top water lures skim the surface of the water to entice fish to grab the bait from the surface of the lake. Top water lures can be quite effective for northern pike, smallmouth bass and largemouth bass. One of the all time favourite brands of top water lures is the Jitterbug.

Fly Fishing

Fly fishing is slowly becoming more popular in Ontario as anglers look to a more challenging method in catching sport fish. Many anglers are put back by the seemingly difficult nature of fly fishing; however, once learned, it is actually quite rewarding. Ardent fly anglers often boast of better success than their spincasting counterparts.

Fly Rods

Rods come in a variety of lengths and weights, depending on your size and the size of the species you intend to fish. As an example, a 9 foot, 6 weight rod would be an ideal set up for everything from bass to trout up to about 5 kg (11 lbs) in size. The heavier the rod, like an 8 weight, the larger the species of fish you can fish for and vice versa. Many experienced fly anglers will have at least two if not three or more rods of different size

and weight in order to maximize their fishing experience. Essentially, the smaller size and weight rod would be used for stream fishing small trout, while the longer heavier rod would be used for bigger species like northern pike or big fighting rainbow trout.

Fly Lines

There are basically three main types of fly lines, floating line, sinking line and sink tip line. Floating line is used to fish top water flies and lures as it sits on top of the water to present the fly on the surface. Sinking line sinks to the depths of the lake in order to present streamer type flies or other subsurface type flies. Sink tip line is a combination of sinking and floating line where just the end of the fly line sinks. This type of line has a number of advantages, one being the ability to present sub surface flies while retaining the visibility of the fly line on the surface. This helps dramatically in spotting strikes, especially when fishing for trout.

Trout Flies

A few of the more popular trout flies used on Kawartha area lakes are the Muddler Minnow, leech patterns and the multi purpose nymph. The Muddler Minnow is the pattern made famous in Ontario for its success with brook trout in the province. The Muddler Minnow imitates a minnow in distress, the ideal meal for a big brookie. Leeches are an intregal part of lake environments in the Kawarthas and are a good fly for slow trolling the deeper portions of lakes, especially in summer when trout are holding deep. Various nymph patterns imitate larvae found in lakes and are the main food source for most trout, especially rainbow and brook trout. It is best to try to match hatch as every lake in the Kawarthas region are full of various insect larvae. Favourite patterns include the various caddis fly stages, mosquitos and damsel fly larvae.

Fly fishing is not a popular method for lake trout, although during spring it can be quite productive. Streamer pattern flies that imitate baitfish can be great for attracting lake trout and the catch of a lifetime.

Bass and Pike Flies

The most exciting fly pattern used for both northern pike and bass is the popper. Poppers are surface flies that can be found in a variety of colours, patterns and sizes. Poppers hop along the top of the water and are great at stirring up aggressive bass and pike. Streamer patterns in colours such as white, red and yellow can also produce for both species. Many bass and pike streamer patterns are often tied with a weedless hook to aid travel through weed areas where many of the big ones hide out. A smallmouth bass fly that is quickly attracting acclaim is the crayfish pattern. Crayfish are tied many different ways but when worked off bottom areas with a sinking line the results can be quite surprising.

Trolling

Trolling can be a very effective angling method, especially on larger water bodies. Trolling covers large areas of water, increasing your chances of finding success on a lake. Trolling is most often used when fishing for larger species, such as lake trout, northern pike, walleye and muskellunge. That does not mean the odd bass will not hit your line.

Trolling speeds should vary to find an effective presentation. Even slow wind drifts should be considered. Trolling along drop-off areas in lakes usually increases your chances significantly. Also, try just along weed lines, as species such as walleye often cruise these areas in search of food. Spoons and plugs are the more popular lures when trolling. Variations such as a worm harness should not be ruled out.

For deep trolling, as is often required during the summer for lake trout, down rigging equipment is required. With the aid of a heavy weight, a downrigger will drop your line and lure to a desired depth in the lake. This enables you to troll your lure through trout holding areas. Down riggers are more common on large water bodies, such as Lake Simcoe.

Ice Fishing

The ice fishing opportunities in the Kawartha region vary depending on the lake. Due to heavy fishing pressure, many lakes in the region have been permanently closed to ice fishing. There still remains a good selection of lakes to ice fish.

The standard set up for ice fishing involves a jig head and a minnow. This method is often productive for all species but it has its limitations. Another popular method is jigging small spoons and other attractant lures. Typically, this method does not produce plenty but it produces the big fish repeatedly. If you do use live bait, be sure to check the regulations, as some lakes in the region have live bait ban restrictions in effect.

Ice fishing season typically begins on January 1st and ends around mid March. Under the general regulations for the region, the main sport fish species available for ice fishing are walleye, northern pike, trout, splake and whitefish. Be sure to check the regulations before heading out as restrictions are continually being revised on a number of lakes, especially lakes with lake trout and walleye populations.

Please Note: There are angling regulations in effect on all water bodies in Ontario in order to preserve the future of the resource. Some of the more specific regulations may include bait bans, special limits, slot size restrictions and closures. Penalty for breaking these regulations can include heavy fines, seizure of equipment and/or imprisonment. Always check the annual Ontario Recreational Fishing Regulations Summary before fishing!

Anstruther Lake

Access

Anstruther Lake is part of the series of lakes in the Kawartha Highlands. The larger lake is found not far off Highway 28 north of Lakefield. Just south of Apsley off Highway 28, Anstruther Lake Road leads west. The road is well marked and should not be difficult to find. Follow Anstruther Lake Road west all the way to the public access area along the east side of Anstruther Lake. The access area is a rough boat launch complete with a parking area.

Lake Definition

Mean Depth:	22 m (72.2 ft)
Max Depth:	39 m (128 ft)
Way Point:	44° 45' 00" Lat - N
	78° 12' 00" Lon - W

Fishing

This large cottage destination lake makes a scenic backdrop for several cottages and offers fishing opportunities for a range of sport fish. Fishing is best for bass as success can be good at times for decent sized smallmouth and largemouth bass. Bass can be found in any of the quiet bays found around the lake. Another good spot to look for bass is around cottage docks and other shore structure.

Unknown to many visitors to Anstruther Lake, the lake is home to a naturally reproducing strain of lake trout. These lakers have been fished heavily in the past but the increased use of catch and release has helped maintain the current lake trout populations. To further help protect the lake trout stocks, the lake is part of the winter/spring fishing sanctuary. Fishing success peaks just after the season opens in late spring. During the summer, down rigging equipment is required to find lake trout. At this time, a good region to try is in the deep area found in the southwest end of the lake. The shoals in this area often hold summer lake trout.

Facilities

Anstruther Lake is home to the well-established public boat access as well as a small marina. West of the main public access, there is another boat launch and marina. The lake also provides access to two fabulous canoe route systems that continue north and south to other lakes in the area. Paddlers looking for Crown Land areas to camp at will find Crab Lake to the south and Rathburn Lake to the north are better suited for camping.

Other Options

A good fishing alternative to Anstruther Lake is **Rathburn Lake**, which is found to the north. The lake is part of the Serpentine Lake Canoe Loop and is accessible via a 162 m (531 ft) portage from the north side of Anstruther Lake. Fishing in Rathburn Lake is rumoured to be decent lake largemouth and smallmouth bass. The lake is also home to a natural population of walleye and is regularly stocked with lake trout.

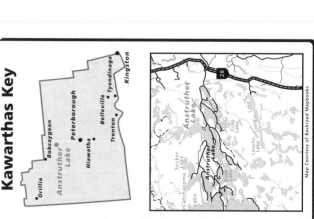

Kawarthas Key

Map Courtesy of Backroad Mapbooks

Apsley Lake

Access

To find Apsley Lake, follow Highway 28 north from Peterborough to the County Road 504 cut-off and the small town of Apsley. Continue east on the 504 to a crossing of Apsley Creek, which can be paddled north to Apsley Lake.

Facilities

There are no facilities available at Apsley Lake, although **Silent Lake Provincial Park** is mere minutes away along Highway 28 north. The park offers full amenities including flush toilets and showers. There are also a few local private campgrounds and tent & trailer parks found in the area. Chandos Lake to the north and Jack Lake to the south are both home to private campgrounds.

Fishing

Apsley Lake is one of those small lakes that can surprise an angler at times. The lake provides fair fishing for smallmouth bass that can be picked up pretty much anywhere around the lake. There are also rumours of the odd largemouth bass being caught in the lake. One particular area to concentrate your efforts is the drop-off area along the western shore of the lake. Some nice sized bass are regularly caught in this area. During slower periods, try working a jig or similar bait close to the bottom.

A unique attraction about Apsley Lake is that the lake supports a small muskellunge population. The musky are not usually very big, but musky hunters may find this lake quite an interesting lake to fish. The deep 12 m (40 ft) holes along with the definite 6 m (20 ft) shoal area make interesting structure to find muskellunge.

Other Options

There are several fine angling alternatives available in the immediate area. The closest lake, Lower Apsley Lake, lies to the southwest of Apsley Lake and is accessible off County Road 504. The lake offers fishing opportunities for both smallmouth and largemouth bass.

Lake Definition

Mean Depth: 5 m (16.4 ft)
Max Depth: 12 m (40.4 ft)
Way Point: 44° 46' 00" Lat - N
78° 04' 00" Lon - W

Kawarthas Key

Map Courtesy of Backroad Mapbooks

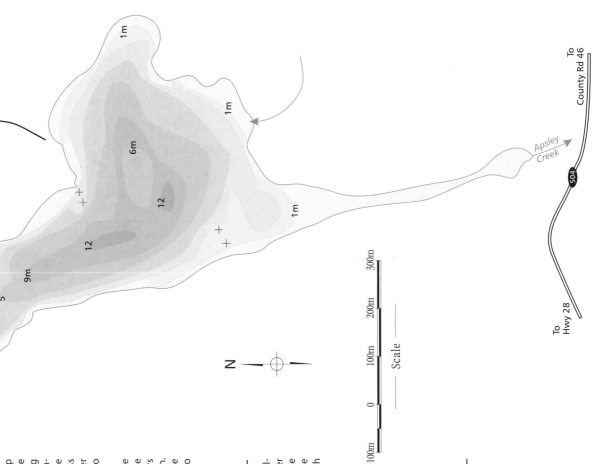

N

Scale

100m 0 100m 200m 300m

Balsam Lake

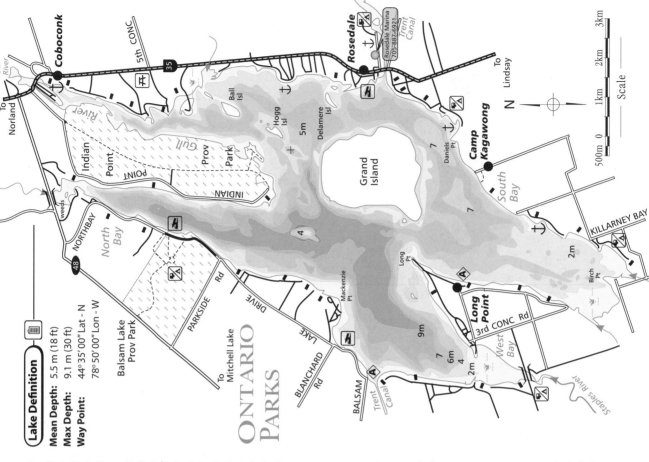

Lake Definition

Mean Depth: 5.5 m (18 ft)
Max Depth: 9.1 m (30 ft)
Way Point: 44° 35' 00" Lat - N
78° 50' 00" Lon - W

Balsam Lake Prov Park

ONTARIO PARKS

Access

The easiest way to find Balsam Lake is to take Highway 35 north from Highway 401. Highway 35 leads directly past the eastern shore of Balsam Lake providing access to all the local boat launches and marinas. Alternatively, you can take County Road 45 east from Highway 12 to access the west side of the lake.

Facilities

Balsam Lake is one of the larger Kawartha Lakes along the Trent-Severn Waterway. There are a few full service marinas and boat launches available. Overnight facilities include a number of tent and trailer parks along with the **Balsam Lake Provincial Park**. The provincial park is a full service park, offering all the basic amenities including flush toilets and showers. The park is very busy throughout the summer months and it is recommended to make reservations prior to arrival. For supplies and other accommodations such as motels, the towns of Coboconk and Fenelon Falls are both within minutes of the lake. For provincial park reservations call (888) ONT-PARK.

Fishing

As one of the more popular Trent-Severn Waterway lakes, Balsam Lake receives significant angling pressure throughout the season, especially during the summer months. Despite the heavy fishing pressure, the lake continues to produce decent results for several sport fish.

Walleye are the main species sought after in the lake and fishing for walleye can be good at times. One area in particular to concentrate efforts is the 4 m (13 ft) shoal hump found in the western portion of the lake. This hump is a natural attractant for weed growth and baitfish, which the predatory walleye mainly feed on. Anglers should also look for other shoal areas that walleye will congregate at in search of easy meals. Alternatively, the various stream mouths found around Balsam are decent holding areas for early season walleye as well as the elusive muskellunge. Musky hunters boast that the lake is quite productive for good-sized muskellunge. In order to maintain the fishery, there have been several regulation changes including reduced limits and slot sizes for walleye.

Largemouth bass and smallmouth bass are the other main sport fish found in Balsam Lake. Good numbers of bass can be found anywhere from the weedy shoreline areas to the rocky shoals bordering the islands around the lake. In fact, the South Bay is a well-known largemouth bass holding area. Top water flies and lures can be a lot of fun in the bay for largemouth during overcast periods or at dusk. As on any lake, bass can become lethargic at times, especially during the heat and bright of summer. To entice these reluctant bass, try working grub type bait such as a jig in a much slower fashion along the bottom structure of known holding areas. Often the less aggressive bass will suck in a well-presented jig as it is worked through their holding area.

Other Options

Cameron Lake to the east is the closest fishing alternative and offers similar fishing opportunities as Balsam Lake. For the more adventurous, the smaller lakes named Raven Lake and Talbot Lake to the east and north are easily accessible from Balsam Lake. Both lakes offer fishing for largemouth and smallmouth bass.

Kawarthas Key

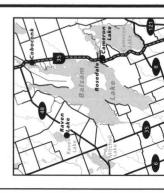

Map Courtesy of Backroad Mapbooks

Bass Lake

Access

The easiest way to access Bass Lake is to travel northeast along County Road 36 from the town of Lindsay through the town of Bobcaygeon. Look for the 17th Concession Road and follow this road north past Nogies Marsh eventually reaching Nogies Creek Road. Nogies Creek Road traverses to the east side of Bass Lake and a rough boat launch area.

Fishing

Bass Lake is inhabited by both smallmouth bass and largemouth bass. Even though there are a number of cottages on Bass Lake, the fishing remains constant, providing generally fair fishing for bass.

The lake has productive weed growth, providing good cover for bass. For this reason, top water presentations can create a stir on the lake at times. Try just off the small island found southwest of the boat launch for ambush ready bass.

There is also a small population of muskellunge found in Bass Lake, although fishing is usually slow. The odd lunker is caught each year.

Other Options

Concession Lake to the east of Bass Lake is accessible by 4wd type trails and offers fishing opportunities for smallmouth and largemouth bass as well as for stocked lake trout. Due to the rough access to the lake, fishing remains fairly steady.

Facilities

The closest facilities to Bass Lake can be found in the town of Bobcaygeon. The town offers a number of private campgrounds as well as a few motels in the area. If you prefer, **Balsam Lake Provincial Park** is located west of Bass Lake, just outside of the town of Coboconk.

Lake Definition

Elevation: 244 m (800 ft)
Surface Area: 115.4 ha (285 ac)
Perimeter: 8.25 km (5.13 mi)
Way Point: 44°41'00"Lat - N
78°32'00"Long - W

Kawarthas Key

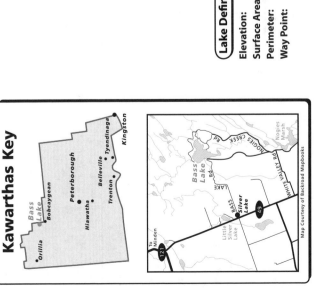

Orillia
Bass Lake
Bobcaygeon
Peterborough
Hiawatha
Belleville
Trenton
Tyendinaga
Kingston

To Minden
121
Little Silver Lake
BASS LAKE Rd
Silver Lake
49
WHITE VALLEY Rd
NOGIES CREEK Rd
Bass Lake
Nogies Marsh

Map Courtesy of Backroad Mapbooks

Bass Lake Map

To Nogies Creek Rd

9
6
1m
3
6m
3
3
3

N

Scale
100m 0 100m 200m 300m 400m 500m

9 3
6
1m

Bass Lake Dam

Nogies Creek

BASS LAKE Rd
To Silver Lake

To Nogies Creek Rd & Concession 17

Bay of Quinte: Picton Area

Access

If you were travelling from Lake Ontario to the Trent Severn Waterway, the Picton portion of the Bay of Quinte would be your first encounter with the big bay. The main access area to this portion of the bay is from the town of Picton. Picton is a scenic, original loyalist community that is easy to find along Highway 33. Highway 33 is essentially an eastern extension of Highway 62, which is accessible from the city of Belleville.

Fishing

The Bay of Quinte is synonymous with fishing. The bay has long been home to fine catches of everything from bass to pike but is best known for its walleye. The bay around the Picton area is not as popular as some of the other regions, although the fishing remains productive. Fishing for walleye can be good at times, while success is usually always better for smallmouth bass or even largemouth bass. Since so many anglers visit the Bay of Quinte for its famed walleye, species such as bass, are often overlooked and underutilized.

Northern pike are also an often ignored sport fish found in the bay. Some big northerns can be hooked in the Bay of Quinte and the word is slowly getting out. Some of the more productive areas for all three sport fish species are found in the Mohawk Bay area and the Hay Bay region. As with most other water bodies, success is often linked to finding underwater structure. Look for shoal areas and weed growth to increase your success, especially for walleye.

Facilities

As a popular boating and vacationing spot, there are numerous facilities available around this portion of the Bay of Quinte. The town of Picton is a beautiful bay side town complete with numerous amenities, including grocery stores, bed and breakfasts, motels and other retail establishments. Outside of the Picton area, you can find a number of different access areas around the bay as well as a few marinas and facilities like tent and trailer parks.

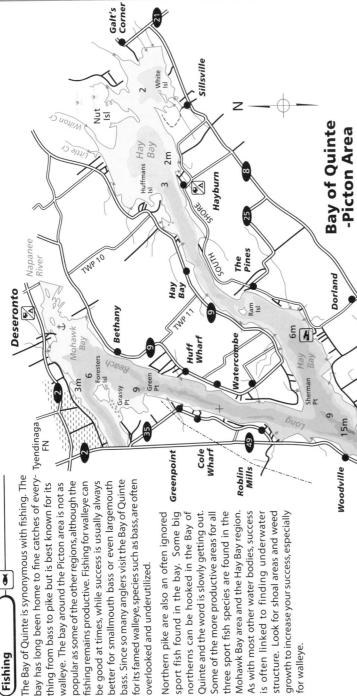

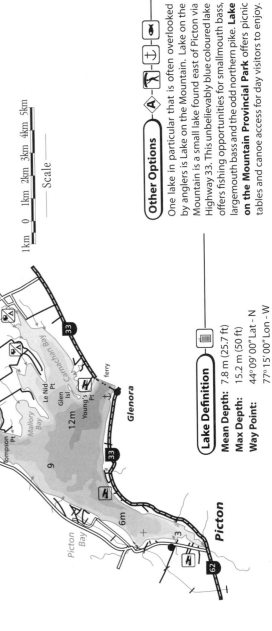

Other Options

One lake in particular that is often overlooked by anglers is Lake on the Mountain. Lake on the Mountain is a small lake found east of Picton via Highway 33. This unbelievably blue coloured lake offers fishing opportunities for smallmouth bass, largemouth bass and the odd northern pike. **Lake on the Mountain Provincial Park** offers picnic tables and canoe access for day visitors to enjoy.

Lake Definition

Mean Depth: 7.8 m (25.7 ft)
Max Depth: 15.2 m (50 ft)
Way Point: 44°09'00" Lat - N   77°15'00" Lon - W

Kawarthas Key

Bay of Quinte: Trenton Area

Access

This portion of the Bay of Quinte is the most northern stretch of the bay and is mainly accessed from the town of Trenton or the city of Belleville. Both areas can be easily reached via Highway 401. The launching area in Belleville is near the northwest side of the Bay Bridge in the southern core of the city. The main access areas in Trenton are located south of the town off the east side of County Road 33.

Fishing

Due to the easy access to this portion of the Bay of Quinte, this area is probably the most popular section of the bay. Every year anglers flock to the bay in search of the fabled walleye fishing. These same anglers often ignore the other species found in the bay. Fishing for walleye can be productive throughout the season, as the shallow, weedy nature of this portion of the Bay of Quinte provides a good source of habitat.

Due to the weed growth and other structure in this part of the bay, bass fishing can be quite good on occasion. Look for rocky shoal areas for smallmouth, while largemouth bass and smallmouth bass can be found anywhere around weed structure.

Northern pike are another great sport fish in the Bay of Quinte that can provide good action at times. Look for pike in the morning or at dusk around weed beds when they cruise the shallows in search of prey.

Other Options

If you are a big water type angler, the best fishing alternative to the Bay of Quinte in this region would be **Lake Ontario**. The expanse of Lake Ontario is accessible to the west of Trenton by vehicle or by boat via the Murray Canal. A large watercraft is needed to fish the lake, as trolling is the main method of angling. Salmon and rainbow trout are the focus of fishing in the giant lake, although you can experience good success for bass and northern pike closer to shore. If your luck is slow, try the many bays along the shore for the abundance of pan fish like crappie and rock bass.

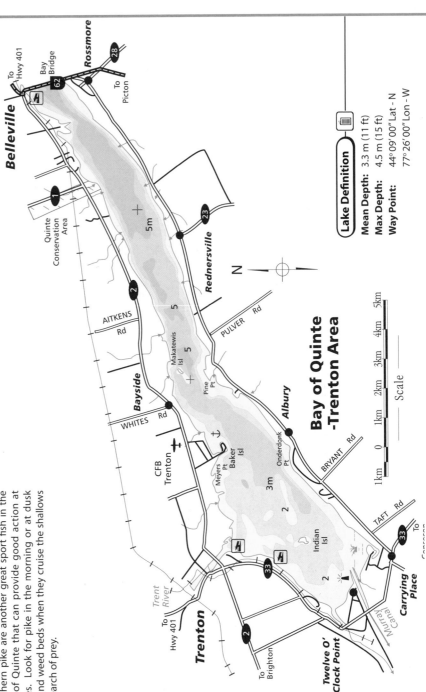

Bay of Quinte -Trenton Area

Lake Definition

Mean Depth: 3.3 m (11 ft)
Max Depth: 4.5 m (15 ft)
Way Point: 44° 09' 00" Lat - N
77° 26' 00" Lon - W

Kawarthas Key

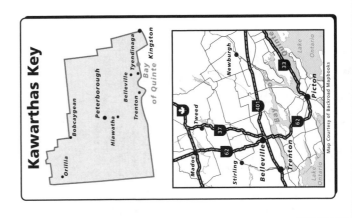

Bay of Quinte: Belleville Area

Access

What is known as the Big Bay, this portion of the Bay of Quinte is mainly accessed from the city of Belleville. There are also other access areas around the bay on Big Island and near the settlements of Northport. Belleville can be found via Highway 401.

Other Options

A few angling alternatives in the area other than the Bay of Quinte are the Salmon River and the Moira River. Both rivers are readily accessible and offer fishing opportunities for mainly bass and pan fish. Watch for sanctuary areas or special restrictions on the **Moira and Salmon Rivers.**

Fishing

Due to the close proximity of this area to the city of Belleville, this is another popular fishing region along the Bay of Quinte. Big Bay is perhaps the most famous angling area as the bay is notorious for producing some good sized walleye. The deeper areas near Northport are also popular angling locations. For smallmouth bass, largemouth bass and northern pike, Muscote Bay is a good choice. The shallow nature of the bay coupled with the usually good weed structure makes for great bass and pike habitat. Of course, you can always find walleye in these type of areas as well. The inlet areas around the Moira River and Salmon River are often decent holding regions for walleye during various portions of the season. Locating the shoal areas around the Salmon River can definitely increase your chances of success.

Facilities

For campers, there are a few tent and trailer parks available on the Tyendinaga First Nations Reserve found east of Belleville. Motels, grocery stores and other amenities are readily found in the city of Belleville. If you prefer, there are the odd bed and breakfast that can be found in the smaller villages like Crofton.

Lake Definition

Mean Depth: 4 m (13.1 ft)
Max Depth: 6 m (19.7 ft)
Way Point: 44°09'00" Lat - N
77°18'00" Lon - W

Bay of Quinte - Belleville Area

Kawarthas Key

Map Courtesy of Backroad Mapbooks

Beaver Lake

Access

Beaver Lake is another fine fishing lake found in the Kawartha Highlands. This area can be busy with boat traffic and is part of a series of canoe routes. To reach the lake, follow County Road 36 north from the town of Buckhorn to Flynn's Turn and head north along County Road 507. County Road 507 passes by the west side of Mississagua and Catchacoma Lakes, which are home to access points to the lake chain. The interconnected chain of lakes include Mississagua, Catchacoma, Gold and Beaver Lakes.

Facilities

The boat launch onto Cavendish Lake is the main access point for Beaver Lake. A marina, boat launch and tent and trailer park can also be found on Catchacoma Lake to the west of Beaver Lake. Beaver Lake is accessible via boat from Catchacoma, Mississagua and Gold Lakes.

Fishing

You can find fair numbers of largemouth and smallmouth bass in Beaver Lake. Bass provide the bulk of the fishing opportunities on the lake and are generally located along almost any of the rocky shoreline or weed structure areas. Off Maniece Island is a known holding area for bass, while the 1-4 m (3-10 ft) shoal area in the middle of the lake almost always produces bass.

A natural population of lake trout also exists in Beaver Lake and the lake is part of the winter/spring fishing sanctuary in order to protect the low lake trout stocks. Lake trout can be caught by trolling during the open season and are usually around the deeper 18 m (59 ft) hole found in the lake. Be sure to practice catch and release whenever possible.

Other Options

The closest angling alternative to Beaver Lake is **Catchacoma Lake** to the west. The bigger lake offers consistent fishing for smallmouth bass, largemouth bass and the odd resident lake trout.

Lake Definition

Elevation:	167.0 m (548 ft)
Surface Area:	529 ha (1,307 ac)
Mean Depth:	2.4 m (7.9 ft)
Max Depth:	12.0 m (39.3 ft)
Perimeter:	21.0 km (13.1 mi)
Way Point:	44°30'00" Lat - N
	77°02'00" Lon - W

To Kawartha Highlands Prov Park

N

BEAVER LAKE Rd

To County Rd 507

Maniece Isl

7 m

4 m

7 m

4 m

7

7 m

4

1 m

11

15 m

18

4 m

To Cavendish Lake

To Catchacoma Lake

Scale

200m   0   200m   400m   600m   800m   1000m

Kawarthas Key

Orillia
Bobcaygeon
Beaver Lake
Peterborough
Hiawatha
Belleville
Trenton
Tyendinaga
Kingston

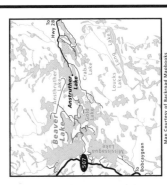

To Hwy 28

Crab Lake
Anstruther Lake
Loucks Lake
Long Lake

Beaver Lake

Mississagua Lake

507

To Bobcaygeon

Map Courtesy of Backroad Mapbooks

15

Belmont Lake

Access

To reach Belmont Lake follow Highway 7 east from Peterborough past the village of Havelock. Just as you are coming out of the village, watch for County Road 48 off the north side of Highway 7. County Road 48 provides access to the southern and eastern portions of the lake. The road also passes over Crowe River. At the bridge a canoe can be launched into the river providing access to the lake.

Facilities

Other than the possibility of renting a cottage on Belmont Lake, there are no facilities available in the immediate area. For cottage rentals, there are a number of resources on the web or inquire with a local real estate agent. All amenities, including groceries, gas, bait can be found in the nearby town of Marmora.

Fishing

Belmont Lake is part of the Crowe River system and offers fishing opportunities for smallmouth bass, largemouth bass, walleye and northern pike. Fishing is best for bass as the weedy and shallow nature of the lake has created some fantastic habitat. While bass can be found away from the weed structure, to find consistent fishing you will need to work your presentation deep into the cover. Working subsurface flies, such as weedless leech or streamer fly patterns, or a tube jig is best to coax these deep holding bass into striking. Look for bass holding in every bay and notably in King Bay, North River Bay and Deer Bay.

Walleye remain a popular sport fish on the lake, while a few northern pike can also be found on occasion. Try trolling worm harnesses or other walleye lures along the weed lines for cruising walleye. A good holding spot is the 6 m (20 ft) shoal found just off the northeast side of Big Island. Reports are that fishing is generally slow to fair for average sized walleye and small pike.

Other Options

Two very close fishing alternatives to Belmont Lake are Round Lake to the west and Crowe Lake to the east. The North River connects Round Lake to Belmont Lake, while the Crowe River flows out of Belmont Lake into Crowe Lake. Both lakes offer decent fishing opportunities for smallmouth and largemouth bass as well as for walleye. Crowe Lake also supports a northern pike population.

Lake Definition

Elevation:	187.0 m (613 ft)
Surface Area:	758 ha (1,872.8 ac)
Mean Depth:	6.2 m (20 ft)
Max Depth:	16.1 m (51 ft)
Way Point:	44° 31' 00" Lat - N
	77° 49' 00" Lon - W

Kawarthas Key

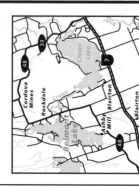

Map Courtesy of Backroad Mapbooks

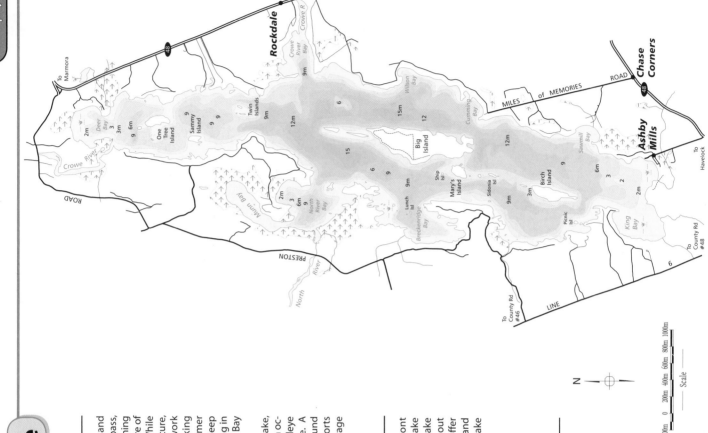

Big & Little Bald Lakes

Access

Both Big Bald and Little Bald Lakes lie south of County Road 36 east of the town of Bobcaygeon. The lakes are accessible via cottage roads that branch south off the county road. The main access road to the lakes is Northern Avenue, which can be picked up via Kennedy or Nichols Cove Roads from County Road 36.

Fishing

The Bald Lakes are just a northern extension of Pigeon Lake; therefore, the fishing quality of the lakes is quite similar. The most predominant sport fish found in the lakes are both smallmouth and largemouth bass. The shallow nature of the lake, coupled with the endless shoal areas, weed lines and underwater rock piles, make for a myriad of bass holding areas in the Bald Lakes. Try off any one of the small islands or in one of the many bays for good bass action throughout much of the season. Topwater lures and flies can be a lot of fun, especially in the quiet bays as dusk approaches.

Walleye and muskellunge also attract a lot of attention throughout the year. Fishing for walleye can be fair to good at times, while angling is slow to fair for musky. The Big Bald Narrows is a known hot spot for walleye, although the sport fish can literally be found throughout the lake. During late spring and summer, weed lines can be a prime holding area for walleye as the predator cruises the structure in search of food. In and around the mouth of the Squaw River is a popular spot to try during the spring opening.

If your luck is slow for the bigger fish, there are always smaller fish to keep you occupied. Sport fish like crappie, perch and rock bass, can be a ton of fun to catch, especially on lighter angling gear.

Facilities

There are no public facilities available on Big Bald Lake or Little Bald Lake; however, there are a number of resorts, motels and private campgrounds in the region that are within easy access to both lakes. Alternatively, **Balsam Lake Provincial Park** lies to the west and offers full facility camping with all the basic amenities of home. The nearby town of Bobcaygeon has numerous retail operations available to supply anything that may be required to make your adventure a success.

Other Options

There are several other fishing options available nearby including a number of large Kawartha Lakes. For a more out of the way alternative, **De Gaulle Lake** and **Concession Lake** to the north offer fishing for bass, while Concession Lake also offers fishing for stocked lake trout. Both lakes are accessed by rough 4wd trails branching off Nogies Creek Road.

Lake Definition

Elevation: 249 m (808 ft)
Mean Depth: 5.2 m (17.7 ft)
Max Depth: 9.2 m (30 ft)
Way Point: 44°34'00"Lat - N 78°23'00"Lon - W

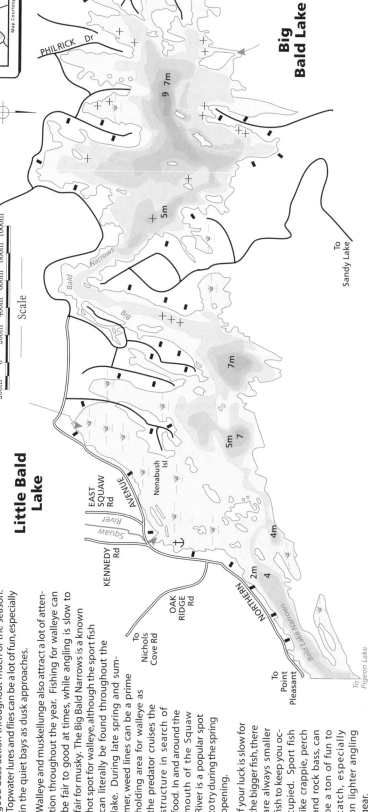

Kawarthas Key

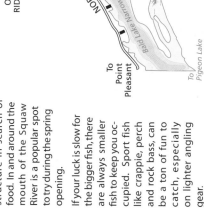

Map Courtesy of Backroad Mapbooks

Big Cedar Lake

Access

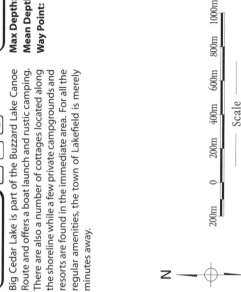

North of the city of Peterborough, you will find Big Cedar Lake by travelling north along Highway 28 past the town of Lakefield to Burleigh Falls. Just northeast of Burleigh Falls, look for Julian Lake Road off the west side of the highway. Julian Lake Road travels past Julian Lake to the boat launch area on Big Cedar Lake.

Other Options

This is a region of seemingly endless lakes and there are plenty to choose from. The chain of lakes found to the north, such as **Coon Lake** and **Buzzard Lake,** offer fishing opportunities for mainly bass. A few of these lakes are stocked with lake trout. Otherwise, **Buckhorn Lake** and **Stoney Lake** to the south are two very popular lakes that can provide a great day worth of fishing.

Fishing

The main sport fish species found in Big Cedar Lake is smallmouth bass, which provide fair to good fishing for nice sized fish. Look for smallmouth off any one of the islands or along drop-off areas. Flipping jigs in deeper water or working spinners in the more shallow areas near structure seem to provide success.

A small population of muskellunge also inhabit the lake but these creatures are very elusive. Although challenging, many musky hunters find success by trolling the lake.

Facilities

Big Cedar Lake is part of the Buzzard Lake Canoe Route and offers a boat launch and rustic camping. There are also a number of cottages located along the shoreline while a few private campgrounds and resorts are found in the immediate area. For all the regular amenities, the town of Lakefield is merely minutes away.

Lake Definition

Max Depth:	18.5 m (61 ft)
Mean Depth:	9.3 m (30.5 ft)
Way Point:	44° 36' 00" Lat - N
	78° 10' 00" Lon - W

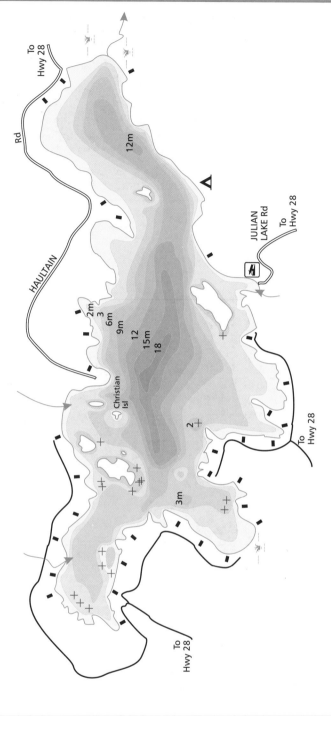

Scale

200m 0 200m 400m 600m 800m 1000m

N

Kawarthas Key

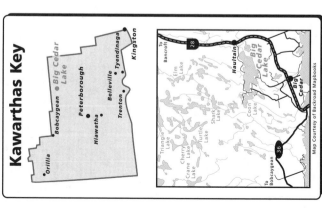

Map Courtesy of Backroad Mapbooks

Bottle Lake

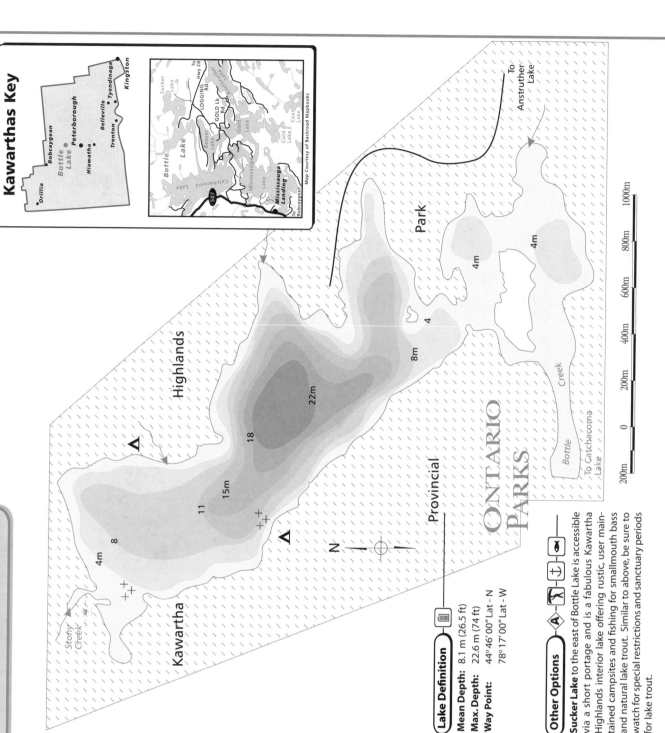

Kawarthas Key

Map Courtesy of Backroad Mapbooks

Access

This scenic lake is part of the original designation of the Kawartha Highlands Provincial Park. The park area has since been expanded substantially creating one of the largest provincial parks in Southern Ontario.

Bottle Lake can be reached by taking County Road 507 off County Road 36 north of the town of Buckhorn. Put in your canoe at one of the Catchacoma Lake boat launch areas and proceed east to Bottle Creek. There is a short portage around the Bottle Creek Dam and it is a short paddle up the creek to reach Bottle Lake.

Fishing

Bottle Lake is actually a fairly deep lake at a maximum depth of approximately 22 m (72 ft) making for suitable habitat for the resident lake trout. The resident lake trout in Bottle Lake are a naturally reproducing strain that has sustained itself into the 21st century. Angling for lakers is generally slow.

Smallmouth bass can provide for good fishing much of the time. A good concentration area for bass is around the creek inlet during the beginning of the season. The rocky drop-off found along the middle portions of the lake also holds smallies. The few small bays along the east side of the lake are also good action areas at times during overcast periods and at dusk.

Even though Bottle Lake is a portage access lake, the lake still receives enough fishing pressure throughout the year to endanger the resident lake trout population. There have been more restrictive regulations and sanctuary periods imposed on the lake to help sustain the natural population. Regardless, the practice of catch and release will go a long way in aiding the trout.

Lake Definition

Mean Depth: 8.1 m (26.5 ft)
Max. Depth: 22.6 m (74 ft)
Way Point: 44°46'00"Lat - N
78°17'00"Lat - W

Facilities

The **Kawartha Highlands Provincial Park** is a non-operating provincial park that was established to help protect some of the wilds of this fascinating portion of the Kawarthas. Facilities at the park are very basic with user maintained, primitive campsites offering rustic fire pits and not much else. Be sure to carry out all off your garbage and leave the campsites cleaner than when you arrive.

Other Options

Sucker Lake to the east of Bottle Lake is accessible via a short portage and is a fabulous Kawartha Highlands interior lake offering rustic, user maintained campsites and fishing for smallmouth bass and natural lake trout. Similar to above, be sure to watch for special restrictions and sanctuary periods for lake trout.

Buckhorn (Upper Buckhorn) Lake

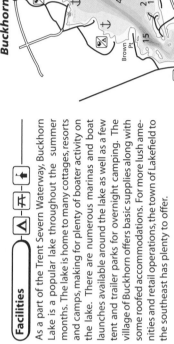

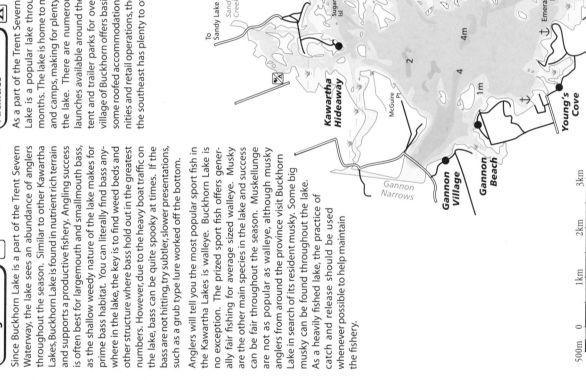

Access

Buckhorn Lake is another famous Kawartha Lake that is a part of the Trent Severn Waterway and can be reached via several different routes. From the south, follow Highway 7A north to Fowler's Corners and County Road 26. County Road 26 travels north to County Road 14, which leads east to County Road 16. County Road 16 can be followed north from County Road 14 providing access to the southwest shore of Buckhorn Lake.

From the east, Highway 134 leads north form Highway 7 just east of Peterborough. Highway 134 eventually changes to Highway 28, which continues north to the village of Burleigh Falls. From Burleigh Falls, take County Road 36 west to the village of Buckhorn on the northeast end of Buckhorn Lake.

Fishing

Since Buckhorn Lake is a part of the Trent Severn Waterway, the lake sees an abundance of anglers throughout the season. Similar to other Kawartha Lakes, Buckhorn Lake is found in nutrient rich terrain and supports a productive fishery. Angling success is often best for largemouth and smallmouth bass, as the shallow weedy nature of the lake makes for prime bass habitat. You can literally find bass anywhere in the lake, the key is to find weed beds and other structure where bass hold out in the greatest numbers. However, due to the heavy boat traffic on the lake, bass can be quite spooky at times. If the bass are not hitting, try subtler, slower presentations, such as a grub type lure worked off the bottom.

Anglers will tell you the most popular sport fish in the Kawartha Lakes is walleye. Buckhorn Lake is no exception. The prized sport fish offers generally fair fishing for average sized walleye. Musky are the other main species in the lake and success can be fair throughout the season. Muskellunge are not as popular as walleye, although musky anglers from around the province visit Buckhorn Lake in search of its resident musky. Some big musky can be found throughout the lake. As a heavily fished lake, the practice of catch and release should be used whenever possible to help maintain the fishery.

Facilities

As a part of the Trent Severn Waterway, Buckhorn Lake is a popular lake throughout the summer months. The lake is home to many cottages, resorts and camps, making for plenty of boater activity on the lake. There are numerous marinas and boat launches available around the lake as well as a few tent and trailer parks for overnight camping. The village of Buckhorn offers basic supplies along with some roofed accommodations. For more lush amenities and retail operations, the town of Lakefield to the southeast has plenty to offer.

Kawarthas Key

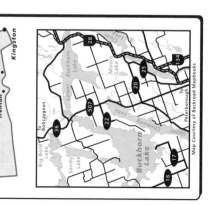

Map Courtesy of Backroad Mapbooks

Buzzard Lake

Access

Buzzard Lake is part of a popular series of canoe access lakes. To reach the chain, follow Highway 28 north from the town of Lakefield past Burleigh Falls to Long Lake Road. Long Lake Road lies off the west side of Highway 28 and leads to the access area on Long Lake. Buzzard Lake is accessible via portage from the southwest end of Long Lake. A marginal fee is charged to park your vehicle at Long Lake Lodge.

Facilities

Buzzard Lake is an interior access lake that is equipped with established rustic campsites. The only development at these sites are a cleared tenting area with a fire pit and possibly a pit toilet. The sites are basic but a great way to rough it and experience some nature. Please remember that these campsites are user-maintained; therefore, leave them as clean or cleaner than when you arrived.

Fishing

Although Buzzard Lake is a canoe access only lake, the lake still receives significant angling pressure. It is an easy day trip from Long Lake, making it a favourite camping/canoeing destination.

Fishing in Buzzard Lake is usually fair for largemouth and smallmouth bass in the 0.5-1 kg (1-2 lb) range. There is plenty of rock structure around the lake that hold smallmouth bass, while largemouth are found predominantly in the quiet shallow bays.

Buzzard Lake is also home to a small population of naturally reproducing lake trout. Lakers were heavily fished in the past by winter ice anglers and new restrictions have been put in place to aid the low stocks. If you do catch a lake trout, the practice of catch and release is recommended to help the stocks recover. Be sure to check the regulations before heading out as Buzzard Lake is part of the winter/spring ice fishing sanctuary and has specific slot size limits on lake trout.

Lake Definition

Max Depth: 41.7 m (137 ft)
Mean Depth: 17.3 m (57 ft)
Way Point: 44°40'00"Lat - N
78°13'00"Lon - W

Other Options

There are a number of different fishing options found around Buzzard Lake. The most obvious option is Long Lake. **Long Lake** offers fishing opportunities for smallmouth bass and natural lake trout. **Vixen Lake** is another nearby lake that is accessible via portage from the southern end of Buzzard Lake. Vixen Lake is known to have a decent smallmouth bass fishery available.

To Long Lake

18m
9m
15
18
21
24
27
30
36
2
3m
6
12m

9
12m
15

9
12m
18m
15
21
2m

2m

To Vixen Lake

N

Scale
100m 0 100m 200m 300m 400m 500m

Kawarthas Key

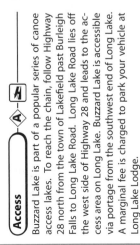

Orillia
Bobcaygeon
Buzzard Lake
Peterborough
Hiawatha
Belleville
Tyendinaga
Trenton
Kingston

Triangle Lake
Cherry Lake
Crane Lake
Turtle Lake
Shark Lake
Buzzard Lake
To Bancroft
28
Elm Lake
Coon Lake
Big Cedar
Long Cedar Lake
Hautain
36
To Bobcaygeon

Map Courtesy of Backroad Mapbooks

Cameron Lake

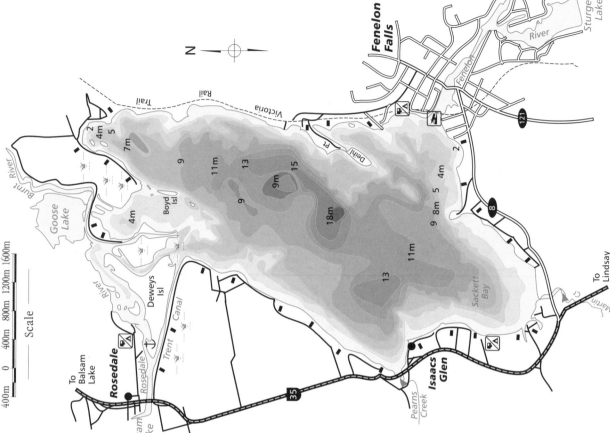

Access

The town of Fenelon Falls is blessed with the scenic backdrop of Cameron Lake. The main access to Cameron Lake is located in Fenelon Falls near the mouth of the Fenelon River and Cameron Lake. To reach Fenelon Falls, travel north from the town of Lindsay along Highway 35 to County Road 121. County Road 121 travels northeast through the downtown core of Fenelon Falls, crossing the Fenelon River along the way.

The lake is also part of the Trent Severn Waterway and many boaters access the lake from the popular water route.

Facilities

Cameron Lake is home to a number of facilities including a boat launch, marina and a few tent and trailer parks. For the explorers at heart, the Victoria Rail Trail traverses along the east side of the lake. The trail is a popular route throughout the year for everything from snowmobiling to hiking. Supplies can be readily found in the town of Fenelon Falls.

Fishing

Cameron Lake is a popular spot for boaters and anglers alike. Fishing in the lake can be good for bass in the 0.5-1 kg (1-2 lb) range. Largemouth bass are the main bass species in Cameron Lake, although smallmouth bass can be found from time to time. Look for largemouth in weedy areas such as in Sackett Bay or around Deweys Island.

Walleye and muskellunge round out the main sport fish species in Cameron Lake. Fishing for walleye can be good at times, while success for muskellunge is usually much slower. Cameron Lake has a very unique lake bottom as it sports a number of different shoal areas of various shapes and depths. The key to increasing your success on this lake is to locate these shoal areas as they regularly hold baitfish that attract sport fish such as walleye and muskellunge.

Other Options

As a part of the Trent Severn Waterway, there are several nearby angling alternatives to Cameron Lake. To the east you will find **Sturgeon Lake** and to the west **Balsam Lake**. Both of these larger lakes are accessible by boat from Cameron Lake and offer similar fishing opportunities. Populations of smallmouth bass, largemouth bass, walleye and muskellunge inhabit these large lakes. If your luck is slow for these more popular species, there is an abundance of other exciting fish to try for, such as crappie, perch or rock bass.

Lake Definition

Max Depth: 18.2 m (60 ft)
Mean Depth: 9.3 m (30.6 ft)
Way Point: 44°33'00"Lat - N
78°46'00"Lon - W

Kawarthas Key

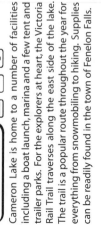

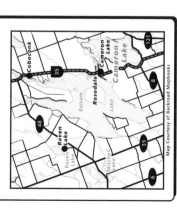

Map Courtesy of Backroad Mapbooks

Canal Lake

Access

This Trent Severn Waterway Lake is found between Lake Simcoe and Balsam Lake. Many boaters access the lake as they travel along the waterway. By land, Canal Lake is found near Highway 12, southeast of Orillia. Follow Highway 12 to the junction with County Road 48 near the small town of Beaverton. Follow County Road 48 east to Centennial Park Road ((County Road 33) and then head north again. Centennial Park Road actually traverses across Canal Lake about 1 km north of the junction with County Road 48.

Fishing

Canal Lake is a very shallow lake with a maximum depth of only 4.6 m (15 ft) and an average depth of approximately 2-3 m (4.5-10 ft). The lake is lush with vegetation throughout the summer months providing ample habitat and cover for all sport fish species. Smallmouth and largemouth bass create most of the fishing action on the lake and can be a lot of fun to catch, especially when they can be convinced to hit surface lures or flies. Surface action is best during overcast periods and in the evening, although the early morning can also be an active period on occasion.

The two most popular sport fish found in Canal Lake are muskellunge and walleye. Fishing for muskellunge is regarded as fair, while success for walleye can be good periodically. Both species reach respectable sizes when compared to the catches in other Trent Severn Waterway lakes. Look for both walleye and musky along weed lines, especially at dusk when they cruise these regions in search of dinner.

Other Options

Nearby **Mitchell Lake** forms part of the Trent Severn Waterway and therefore is accessible by boat from Canal Lake. By vehicle, you can reach Mitchell Lake by continuing east along County Road 48. Fishing in the smaller lake is similar to Canal Lake, as largemouth bass, smallmouth bass, walleye and the ever-predacious muskellunge inhabit the lake.

Lake Definition

Max Depth: 4 m (13.1 ft)
Mean Depth: 3 m (9.8 ft)
Way Point: 44°34'00"Lat - N
79°03'00"Lon - W

Facilities

Along Centennial Park Road (County Road 33) you will pass by a tent and trailer park and a boat launch onto Canal Lake. The boat launch is actually located along the northern shore of the lake, while the trailer park sits on the western shore of the large island. Supplies can be found in the nearby town of Beaverton.

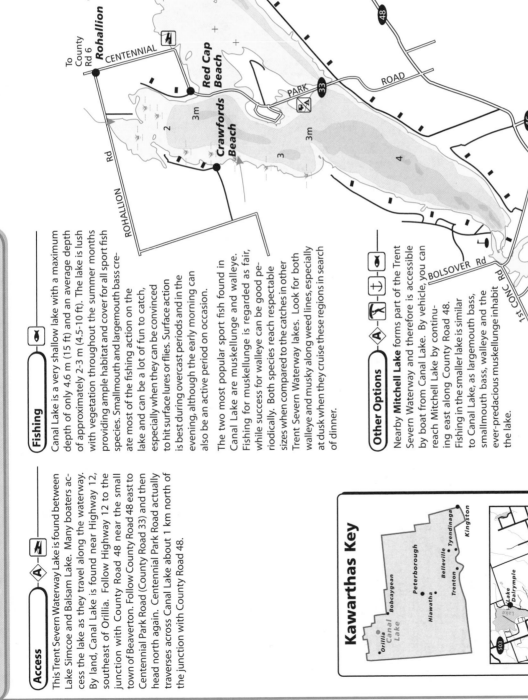

Kawarthas Key

Map Courtesy of Backroad Mapbooks

Chandos Lake

Access

Chandos Lake is found just east of Highway 28 and has several access points. The main public access point is found at the north end of the lake. To find this area, travel north on Highway 28 and take the second Apsley cut-off to County Road 620. Follow this road along the north side of Chandos Lake all the way to the small picnic area and boat launch at the top end of the lake.

Fishing

This popular cottage destination lake is regularly fished throughout the season. Bass, both smallmouth and largemouth, seem to be the most readily caught species. Bass average about 0.5-1 kg (1-2 lbs) although can reach up to 1.5+ kg (3.5+ lbs) in size on occasion. The lake is home to a seemingly endless array of small bays that make for prime bass holding areas.

Chandos Lake is also home to a naturally reproducing strain of lake trout. They and are mainly found in the east portion of the lake where the depths offer a much more suitable habitat for lakers. Trolling is the preferred angling method for lake trout, as the finicky trout is best found by covering large tracts of water. For increased lake trout success, locate the anomalies along the lake bottom such as rock shoals where baitfish will normally congregate.

Lake trout remain under heavy angling pressure in Chandos Lake and the practice of catch and release is recommended. Before heading out, be sure to check your regulations for slot size restrictions and sanctuary periods.

Facilities

There are a few small marinas on Chandos Lake along with a public boat launch and picnic area on the north shore. There are also two private tent and trailer parks found off Balmer Road along the south shore. The nearest provincial park is Silent Lake, which lies to the north off Highway 28 and is a full facility park complete with showers and flush toilets.

Lake Definition

Max Depth: 45.7 m (150 ft)
Mean Depth: 27.1 m (89 ft)
Way Point: 44°49'00" Lat - N
78°00'00" Lon - W

Other Options

To the north of Chandos Lake there are many lakes to choose from, including **Silent Lake** and **Eels Lake**. Silent Lake offers angling for lake trout and bass in a park setting, while Eels Lake provides fishing opportunities for smallmouth bass, walleye and lake trout.

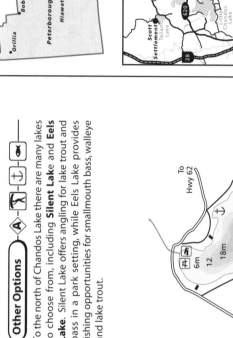

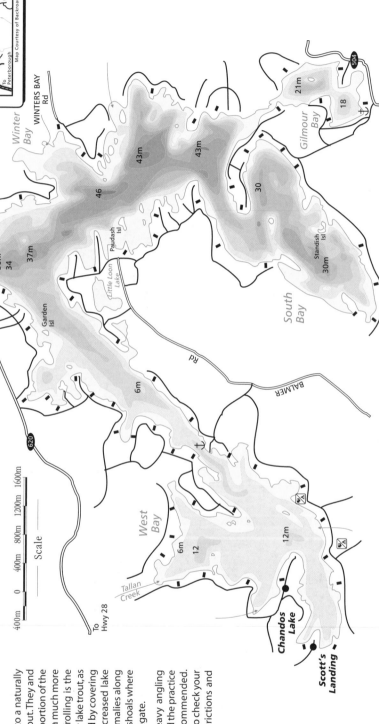
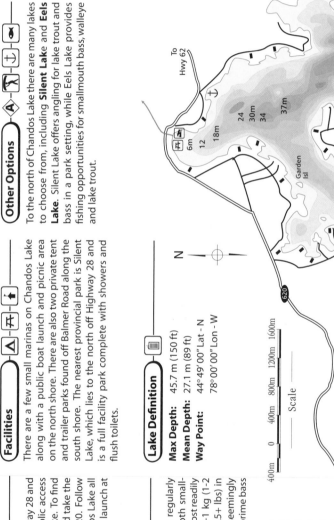

Chemong (Upper Chemong) Lake

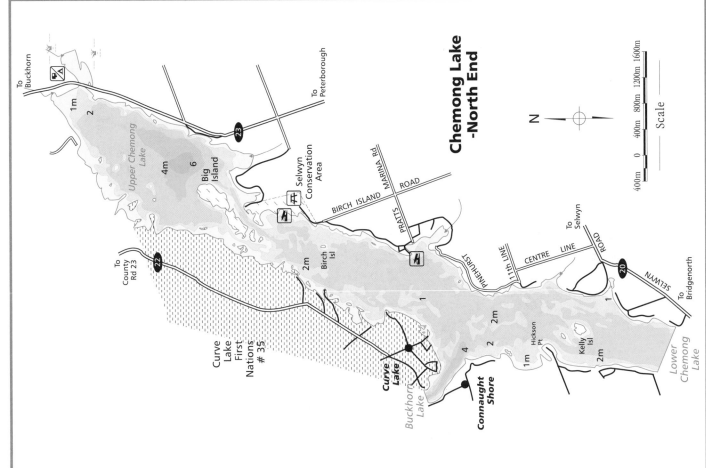

Access (north) 🅰 ⚡

A popular access spot to Upper Chemong Lake is from the public boat launch at the Selwyn Conservation Area. To find the conservation area, follow County Road 29 north from Peterborough to County Road 23. Take County Road 23 northwest all the way to the settlement of Selwyn. At the four-way junction in Selwyn, turn west along Pratts Marina Road to Birch Island Road. Travel north along Birch Island Road to the conservation area. If you prefer, there is also another boat access just south of the conservation area off the end of Pratts Marina Road.

Fishing 🐟

Although Chemong Lake is officially part of the Trent Severn Waterway lakes, the lake is not a part of the main travel route and hence receives somewhat lower boating traffic than other Trent Severn Lakes. Fishing in the long lake is best for smallmouth and largemouth bass, while walleye fishing is generally fair.

Due to its shallow nature, Chemong Lake is quite weedy providing plenty of superb habitat for all fish species. Look for weed lines around the lake to help increase your success. A productive method in finding walleye on this lake is to troll along weed lines with a worm harness tipped with a worm. The attractant of the spinners on the lure grab the attention of walleye, while the worm is often the key ingredient to enticing the strike. With all the weed structure it can be difficult at times to know if you have a hit or not. It takes some practice in knowing the difference between a good weed tug and a walleye strike in the Kawartha Lakes. A fair population of muskellunge also inhabits Chemong Lake. Watch for sanctuary areas.

Facilities (north) 🛆 🏕 🚻

The **Selwyn Conservation Area** located along the eastern shore of the lake is a popular summer spot for visitors. The conservation area offers a boat launch, picnic area, beach and trail systems. The park is also available for camping for groups by reservation only. Call (705) 745-5791 or (705) 652-8831 for more information.

Along with the conservation area a number of facilities are available on the north end of Chemong Lake. These facilities include a tent and trailer park found on the north shore as well as a small marina and boat launch south of the conservation area.

Kawarthas Key

Map Courtesy of Backroad Mapbooks

Chemong (Lower Chemong) Lake

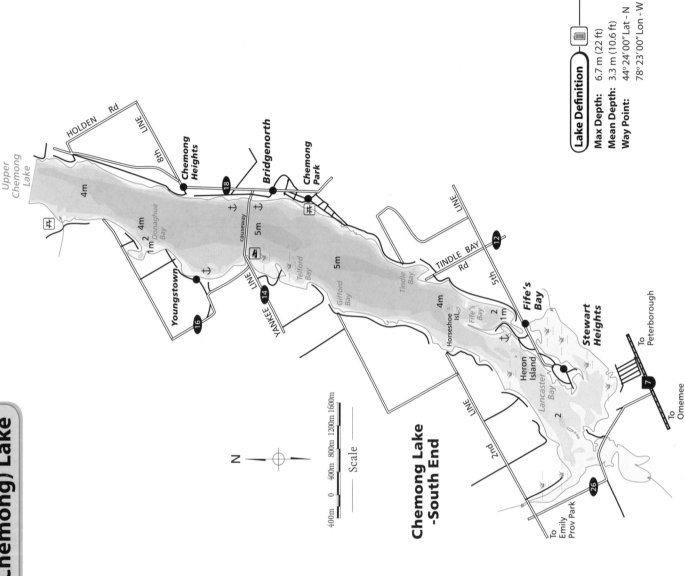

**Chemong Lake
-South End**

Scale
400m 0 400m 800m 1200m 1600m

N

Lake Definition

Max Depth:	6.7 m (22 ft)
Mean Depth:	3.3 m (10.6 ft)
Way Point:	44° 24' 00" Lat - N
	78° 23' 00" Lon - W

Access (south)

The South End of Chemong Lake lies just to the west of the city of Peterborough. The village of Bridgenorth is a popular access point and can be found via County Road 18. You can find County Road 18 by following County Road 1 west from Highway 7 at Fowlers Corner.

Other Options

The closest angling alternative to Chemong Lake is the neighbouring Buckhorn Lake. **Buckhorn Lake** is connected to the western shore of Chemong Lake and is part of the main Trent Severn Waterway. Regardless of the increased boat activity, Buckhorn Lake offers good angling opportunities for its resident largemouth bass, smallmouth bass, walleye and muskellunge.

Lake Definition

Bridgenorth has plenty to offer Chemong lake visitors, including easy access to supplies and other amenities, such as lodging. Marinas can be found in Bridgenorth, near Fife's Bay as well as near the settlement of Youngstown. There is also a boat launch available across the causeway from Bridgenorth on the west side of Chemong Lake.

Cherry Lake

Kawarthas Key

Map Courtesy of Backroad Mapbooks

Access

Cherry Lake lies within the potential future boundary of the Kawartha Highlands Provincial Park and is part of the Turtle Lake Canoe Route. The lake is only accessible via portage from either Triangle Lake to the north or Turtle Lake to the south.

The main canoe access area for this group of lakes is found at the east end of Long Lake. Long Lake can be reached by travelling north along Highway 28 past Lakefield to Long Lake Road off the west side of the highway. From the highway, it is a short drive to the access point and parking area at Long Lake Lodge. A small fee may apply for parking.

Fishing

This scenic backcountry lake is a fantastic location to get away from the hustle and bustle of the urban world. Cherry Lake is part of a collection of interconnecting lakes that offer great canoeing possibilities although fishing is generally slow for stocked lake trout. In the past few years, lakers have been stocked to help replenish the ailing stocks. The best time to try for these stocked trout is in the spring just after ice off. In summer, as they revert to the deeper portion of the lake as the heat of summer approaches. Try trolling a small spoon along drop-off areas in spring.

Facilities

There is a camping area and other facilities available at **Long Lake Lodge** at the eastern shore of Long Lake. The lodge also hosts a boat launch and parking area for canoeists. Since the paddle to Cherry Lake is at least a day away, there are several established rustic campsites available on all the nearby lakes. Campsites are user maintained and usually offer only a rough fire pit.

Lake Definition

Max Depth: 18 m (59 ft)
Mean Depth: 6.8 m (22.5 ft)
Way Point: 44° 40' 00" Lat - N
78° 15' 00" Lon - W

Other Options

There are plenty of other angling options available in the nearby area. **Triangle Lake** to the north of Cherry Lake provides fishing for lake trout, while **Turtle Lake** to the south offers angling for smallmouth bass. Other options in the area also include **Cox Lake** to the north and **Stoplog Lake** to the east. Cox Lake is inhabited by smallmouth bass and stocked lake trout, while Stoplog Lake is home to resident lake trout and both smallmouth and largemouth bass.

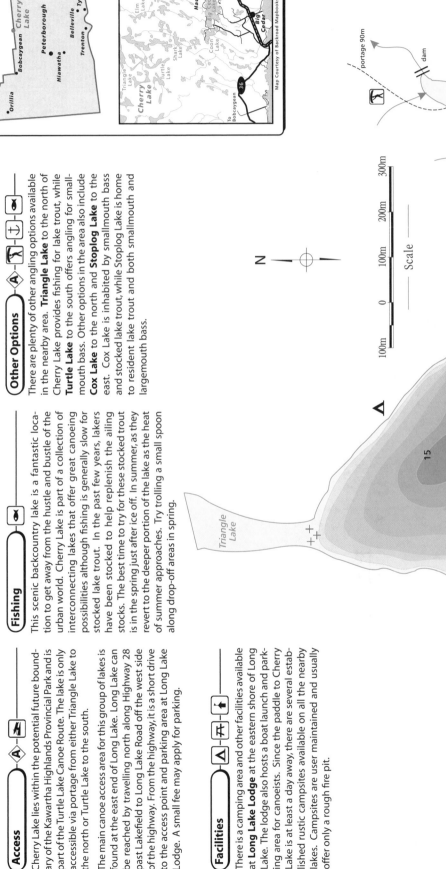

N

Scale

Triangle Lake

To Turtle Lake — portage 117m

portage 90m

dam

Stocking Info

Fish Species	Number
Lake Trout	200

27

Clydesdale Lake

Access

Clydesdale Lake is settled in the rolling hill area north of the town of Apsley. The lake can be reached by following Highway 28 north to County Road 620 at the town of Apsley. Follow County Road 620 north to the lake. A few access roads jut off the north side of County Road 620 that lead to Clydesdale Lake. Watch for private property.

Facilities

There are really no facilities available at Clydesdale Lake, although supplies and accommodations can be found in and around the town of Apsley. For overnight camping, there are two tent and trailer parks on the southern shore of Chandos Lake that are within a short drive from Clydesdale Lake. If you prefer, **Silent Lake Provincial Park** is a little further away, although it can be reached via Highway 28 just north of Apsley.

Fishing

Both largemouth and smallmouth bass inhabit Clydesdale Lake. Fishing for bass can be fair at times and is most productive during overcast periods or at dusk. Clydesdale Lake is a shallow body of water with and average depth of only about 2 m (6.5 ft). The shallow nature of the lake helps create the perfect conditions for weed growth that provide cover for bass. Look for bass along weed lines or even underneath weed cover. In heavy weeds, a jig type lure can be worked through the cover and provide fewer snags than spinner type lures. The regions off either one of the small islands are sure to be a holding area for bass.

Other Options

Chandos Lake is located just south of Clydesdale Lake. There is an access area to **Chandos Lake** off the south side of County Road 620 east of Clydesdale Lake. Chandos Lake offers fishing opportunities for largemouth bass, smallmouth bass, northern pike and lake trout. Please practice catch and release whenever possible.

Lake Definition

Max Depth: 3 m (10 ft)
Mean Depth: 2 m (6.5 ft)
Way Point: 44°50'00" Lat - N
78°01'00" Lon - W

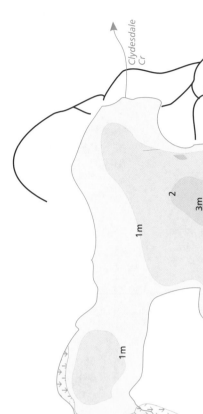

Scale

100m 0 100m 200m 300m 400m 500m

N

Kawarthas Key

Map Courtesy of Backroad Mapbooks

Consecon Lake

Kawarthas Key

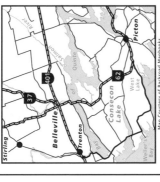

Map Courtesy of Backroad Mapbooks

Access

Consecon Lake is located south of the town of Trenton. To reach the lake, follow Highway 401 to County Road 33 and travel south past the west arm of the Bay of Quinte. County Road 33 eventually leads to the small settlement of Consecon and Consecon Lake.

Facilities

The town of Consecon offers retail facilities supporting all your supply needs such as food and fuel. There are also two private tent and trailer parks located along the northern shore of Consecon Lake. Both parks are accessible via Lakeside Drive east of the settlement of Consecon.

Fishing

Smallmouth bass and largemouth bass provide most of the action on Consecon Lake. Bass can be found throughout the lake, including in the shallow western portion of the lake west of the rail tracks. The lake has a number of established weed areas that also make for prime holding areas for largemouth and the odd smallmouth bass.

Northern pike and walleye are also found in the lake but fishing for both species is merely slow to fair. The area just west of the Melville Creek can be a fair holding area for walleye and northern pike during the early part of the open water season. Trolling a worm harness can be an effective method at times. Try to troll along weed lines for increased success.

Other Options

The two closest and most popular fishing destinations in the area are Lake Ontario and the Bay of Quinte. There are several boat launch areas onto both water bodies or if you require a guide, there are numerous outfitters that will take you out for a day of fishing for a nominal fee. Fishing in Lake Ontario is mainly for big salmon, rainbow trout and the odd lake trout. The Bay of Quinte is famous for its walleye; however, numerous other species can be caught in the bay. Bass and pike can be found in both waters, generally closer to land where shore structure is found.

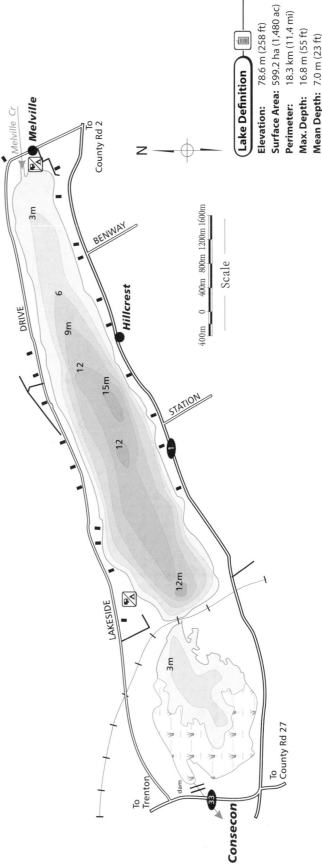

Lake Definition

Elevation:	78.6 m (258 ft)
Surface Area:	599.2 ha (1,480 ac)
Perimeter:	18.3 km (11.4 mi)
Max. Depth:	16.8 m (55 ft)
Mean Depth:	7.0 m (23 ft)
Way Point:	44°00'00" Lat - N 77°27'00" Lon - W

Coon Lake

Access

Coon Lake is found not far from Highway 28 north of Lakefield. To reach the smaller lake, follow Highway 28 north from Lakefield to the settlement of Burleigh Falls. Just north of Burleigh Falls you can find Coon Lake Road off the north side of Highway 28. Follow Coon Lake Road around the east end of Coon Lake to the boat launch area on the east shore.

Facilities

Along with the boat launch, Coon Lake is part of a fantastic canoe route. Coon Lake is sometimes used as the southern access point to the chain or as the first lake in the route beginning from Big Cedar Lake to the east.

Fishing

Coon Lake is home to a number of cottages but the lake seems to avoid the summer vacation rush. Fishing in the lake is regarded as generally fair for its resident smallmouth and largemouth bass. There are a few weedy patches found around the lake that make for good hiding areas for ambush ready largemouth bass. Smallmouth bass can be found in weed cover but also off rocky drop-off around the shoreline. Top water presentations can be effective at times, but spinner baits and jigs seem to be a more productive lure for the bass of Coon Lake.

A population of muskellunge also inhabit the lake and fishing can be fair at times. Seasoned musky anglers will often find that Coon Lake can be a productive muskellunge fishery. Similar to most musky lakes, the action is often best in the late summer to fall period.

Other Options

To the north, you can access **Shark Lake** and a number of other interior canoeing lakes. To reach Shark Lake entails three portages totalling over 2,000 m (6,562 ft) but it is sure worth the trip. Besides the welcomed seclusion, the remote lake offers interior Crown Land camping opportunities. As a bonus, the lake also provides good fishing for smallmouth bass, largemouth bass and stocked splake.

Lake Definition

Max Depth: 15.2 m (50 ft)
Mean Depth: 6.8 m (22.5 ft)
Way Point: 44° 37' 00" Lat - N
78° 12' 00" Lon - W

To Big Cedar Lake

COON LAKE Rd

To Hwy 28

To Shark Lake

2m

3m

9m
12
15m

6

3

2

1m

N

Scale

100m 0 100m 200m 300m 400m 500m

Kawarthas Key

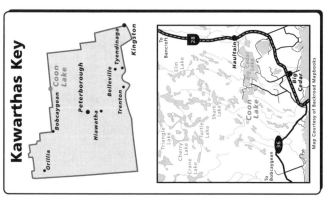

Orillia
Bobcaygeon
Coon Lake
Peterborough
Hiawatha
Belleville
Trenton
Tyendinaga
Kingston

To Bancroft
Elm Lake
Haultain
Big Cedar Lake
Triangle Lake
Cherry Lake
Crane Lake
Turtle Lake
Shark Lake
Coon Lake
Big Cedar
28
36
To Bobcaygeon

Map Courtesy of Backroad Mapbooks

Copper Lake

Access

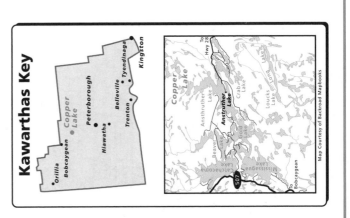

This backcountry fishing lake can be accessed by canoe and a series of portages. To begin the long journey in, you will need to access Anstruther Lake to the south and then Rathburn Lake to the west.

From Highway 28 just south of the cut-off to the town of Apsley, look for the Anstruther Lake Road. Follow this road past a marina before reaching the public access area to Anstruther Lake. There is a canoe put in at the access area, as well as free parking. From the north end of Anstruther Lake a short 162 m (530 ft) portage leads to Rathburn Lake. Paddle to the eastern shore of Rathburn and the mouth of Anstruther Creek. From here you will need to portage and paddle up the creek, eventually meeting the isolated Copper Lake.

Fishing

Since access to Copper Lake is more challenging, the fishing remains decent. As is often the case, the few portages keep the bulk of anglers out of a lake.

Fishing in Copper Lake is known to be good at times for nice sized largemouth bass. The shallow nature of the lake makes for ideal bass habitat and there is plenty of weed growth found around the lake. For fly anglers, top water poppers or even a floating Muddler Minnow can create a real frenzy of action on the lake.

Copper Lake is also inhabited by a marginal population of walleye. Some claim the fishing for walleye can be good, while others have had little or no luck at all for the sharp toothed predator.

Other Options

To access Copper Lake, you must first travel across Rathburn Lake. **Rathburn Lake** is an interior lake that is home to user maintained Crown Land campsites and fishing opportunities for smallmouth bass, largemouth bass, walleye and stocked lake trout.

Lake Definition

Max Depth:	5.4 m (18 ft)
Mean Depth:	4 m (13.1 ft)
Way Point:	44°47'00"Lat - N
	78°10'00"Lon - W

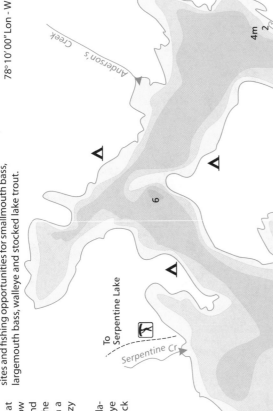

Facilities

Copper Lake is a Crown Land lake that has become a part of the Kawartha Highlands Provincial Park expansion. The park was established to help preserve much of the remote access parts of the region. Currently, Copper Lake offers visitors a few rustic user maintained campsites. The campsites are usually clean and very tranquil. Please be sure to carry any garbage out after your visit to help keep them that way.

The nearest development is on Anstruther Lake. The bigger lake is home to several cottages and a marina. Basic supplies can also be picked up in the town of Apsley.

Kawarthas Key

Map Courtesy of Backroad Mapbooks

Cordova Lake

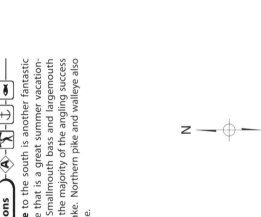

To County Rd 48

VANSICKLE Rd

Crowe River

Dr

McMILLAN

2
3m
6
9m
12

2
3m
6
12
9m
6m
2m
9m
12
6
9m
12

FISH HATCHERY Rd

To Belmont Lake

Belmont Rd

P 100m

Crowe River

dam

Lake Definition

Elevation:	213 m (700 ft)
Surface Area:	11 ha (27.3 ac)
Perimeter:	19.82 km (12.31 mi)
Max Depth:	15 m (49 ft)
Mean Depth:	4.6 m (15 ft)
Way Point:	44°35'00" Lat - N
	77°50'00" Lon - W

Access

Cordova Lake is a popular recreational lake that is frequented by anglers and canoeists. To find the lake, travel east from the city of Peterborough on Highway 7 to the town of Havelock. Just to the east of town, take County Road 48 northeast to Freeman Corners. At Freeman Corners, continue along County Road 48 north past Cordova Mines to Vansickle Road. Follow Vansickle Road north to the access point on the north end of Cordova Lake.

Facilities

There is a tent and trailer park near the north end of Cordova Lake for the campers at heart. Otherwise, there are a few motels available between Marmora to the east and Norwood to the west of Havelock. All three towns offer full services for trip planning and any emergencies.

Fishing

Bass can be readily caught throughout the lake, while pike can be found in the shallows in the spring and just off drop-offs and weed lines in the summer months. Walleye are best found near the Crowe River inlet, especially during the early part of the season. During the rest of the year it is recommended to look for walleye off the shoal areas found throughout the lake. Spinners and jigs are basic lures that can provide success for all three species on this lake. Crankbaits and other similar lures such as rapalas can also be proficient producers on Cordova Lake.

Other Options

Belmont Lake to the south is another fantastic Kawartha Lake that is a great summer vacationing location. Smallmouth bass and largemouth bass make up the majority of the angling success on Belmont Lake. Northern pike and walleye also inhabit the lake.

N

Scale

200m 0 200m 400m 600m 800m 1000m

200m

Kawarthas Key

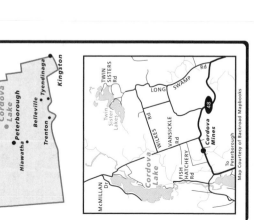

Orillia
Bobcaygean
Cordova Lake
Peterborough
Hiawatha
Belleville
Trenton
Tyendinaga
Kingston

TWIN SISTERS Rd
LONG SWAMP Rd
Rd
48
Twin Sisters Lakes
WILKES Rd
VANSICKLE Rd
Cordova Mines
McMILLAN Dr
Cordova Lake
FISH HATCHERY Rd
To Peterborough

Map Courtesy of Backroad Mapbooks

Crab Lake

Access

Found on the Wolf Lake Canoe Route, Crab Lake is best accessed by boat. The access point to Wolf Lake is found off Anstruther Lake Road, just west of Highway 28. Once on Wolf Lake, it is a short paddle west to the portage to Crab Lake.

Other Options

Some other fishing options in the area include **Wolf Lake** and **Loon Call** Lake to the north and east of **Crab Lake**. Alternatively the much larger Anstruther Lake to the west. All three lakes offer bass fishing. Anstruther Lake has a small lake trout population, while Loon Call Lake is stocked with splake periodically. Musky hunters may find the odd muskellunge in Wolf Lake.

Fishing

Crab Lake is a shallow lake with a maximum depth of 6 m (20 ft), coupled with several shallow bays and inlets. Needless to say, this is prime habitat for lunker bass.

Smallmouth can be readily found throughout the lake, however steady producing areas can be found off the two small islands in the middle of the lake. One spot that should definitely be tried is the 3 m (10 ft) hump in the middle of the northeast portion of the lake. This abnormal structure area is a good attractant for smallmouth.

Facilities

Crab Lake is home to several user maintained, rustic campsites. The campsites are usually made up of a small cleared area and a rough fire pit. The fine sites are great for a mid week camping vacation but can be a little busy on weekends.

Lake Definition

Max Depth: 6.7 m (22 ft)
Mean Depth: 3 m (9.8 ft)
Way Point: 43°44'00" Lat - N 78°12'00" Lon - W

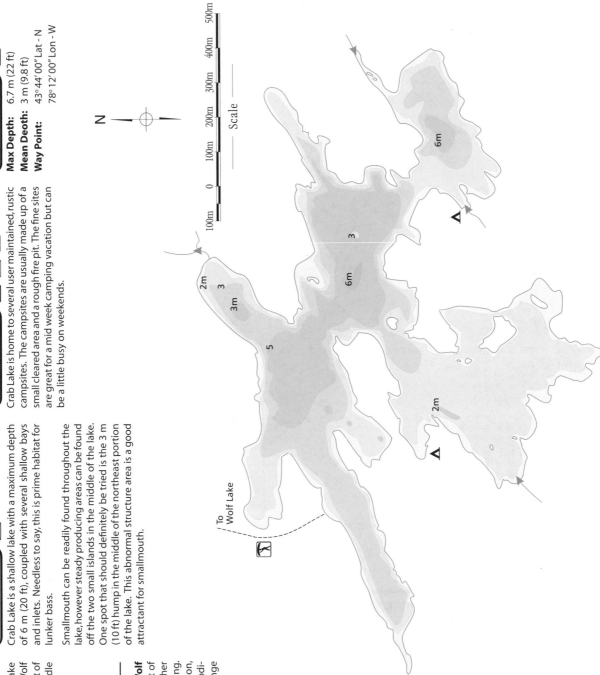

Kawarthas Key

Map Courtesy of Backroad Mapbooks

Crowe Lake

Access

This popular cottage destination lake lies just outside of the town of Marmora. From Highway 7, turn north at the lights onto County Road 33. County Road 33 parallels the east side of the Crowe River and leads directly to Crowe Lake. To reach Marmora, follow Highway 7 east from the city of Peterborough past the town of Havelock.

Fishing

Crowe Lake is a very interesting lake to fish due to the unique contours of the lake bottom. The weedy nature of the lake provides a multitude of structure for bass. In particular, the shoreline area is filled with weed growth and bass sit ambush ready for passing lures. All the typical bass lures will produce on Crowe Lake but, similar to any lake, productivity can definitely be affected by variables such as weather patterns.

The three largest sport fish are walleye, northern pike and muskellunge. Northern pike and muskellunge can be found to good sizes in this lake and can be anywhere from the deeper shoal areas to the shallow weed lines. Spinner baits, spoons and even top water presentations can be successful for northerns. Regular productivity for musky certainly takes some luck and experience, as the big predator can be difficult to find consistently. Walleye fishing certainly draws the most anglers and can be productive at times, although there are periods where walleye can be quite hard to find on Crowe Lake. The deeper holes, where the depth changes dramatically, found around the lake are prime holding areas. Try trolling or jigging off one of the surrounding shoals to attract walleye and other predatory fish. Watch for special size restrictions on muskellunge on Crowe Lake

Facilities

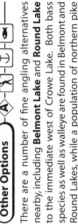

The town of Marmora has plenty of retail options for visitors, including a grocery store and a hardware store for various supplies. The town can be a bustle of activity during the summer months as cottagers flock to the area in search of their summer solace. For overnight camping, there are four tent and trailer parks available on Crowe Lake. Alternatively, there are a few motels off Highway 7 near the town of Marmora.

Other Options

There are a number of fine angling alternatives nearby, including **Belmont Lake** and **Round Lake** to the immediate west of Crowe Lake. Both bass species as well as walleye are found in Belmont and Round Lakes, while a population of northern pike also inhabits Belmont Lake.

Kawarthas Key

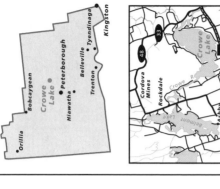

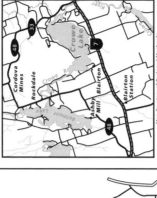

Map Courtesy of Backroad Mapbooks

Lake Definition

Max Depth:	16.4 m (54 ft)
Mean Depth:	10.3 m (34 ft)
Way Point:	44° 29' 00" Lat - N
	77° 44' 00" Lon - W

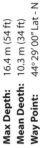

N

Scale

400m 0 400m 800m 1200m 1600m

Crowe River

CONCESSION

Blairton

To Hwy 7

BIG

ISLAND

ROAD

CROWE   LAKE   ROAD

Crowe

River

To Marmora

Marmora Dam

2m

3m

6m

9m

12

15m

15

9

15m

9m

6m

6

2m

34

Crystal Lake

Access ▶ 🅰 ⚡

The southern access route to Crystal Lake begins in the town of Fenelon Falls. To reach Fenelon Falls, follow Highway 35 north of Lindsay to County Road 8. County Road 8 travels east from Highway 35 to Fenelon Falls. Follow the road through the town to County Road 121. If you follow County Road 121 north it will eventually meet Crystal Lake Road. Crystal Lake Road (also known as 11th Concession Road) is a rough 2wd access road that traverses directly to the southern shore of Crystal Lake.

Fishing ▶ 🐟

Crystal Lake is home to several camps and cottages and is regularly fished throughout the year. Smallmouth bass provide the most action on the lake and fishing for the feisty sport fish is generally fair. Look for smallies near cottage dock structures or off any of the small rocky islands found around the lake.

Crystal Lake is also inhabited by natural populations of walleye and lake trout. Fishing for these prized species is fair at best. Walleye anglers should look to shoal areas around the lake to help increase angling success. One spot in particular is the shoal hump found just to the north of the deep 33 m (108 ft) hole located in the middle of the lake.

Overharvesting is the main reason why the fishing quality on is suffering for these sport fish. To help aid the lake trout stocks, special restrictions such as slot size limits have been implemented.

Other Options ▶ 🅰 🍴 ⚓

A few good fishing alternatives can be found south of Crystal Lake via the Forest Access Road. The Forest Access Road can be quite rough in sections and requires a high clearance vehicle. Both Otter Lake and Loom Lake are found next to the logging road and offer Crown Land camping opportunities and fishing for smallmouth bass. **Otter Lake** is also inhabited by a population of muskellunge, while **Loom Lake** supports a small largemouth bass fishery.

Facilities ▶ ⛺ 🏕 ⛪

Crystal Lake offers a boat launch area located along the southern shore off the Crystal Lake Road. Supplies can be found in the town of Fenelon Falls or alternatively in the town of Lindsay. There are a few campgrounds near Fenelon Falls or if you don't mind a longer drive, Balsam Lake Provincial Park lies within minutes west of Fenelon Falls.

Lake Definition 🔲

Max Depth:	33 m (108 ft)
Mean Depth:	19.2 m (63 ft)
Way Point:	44° 46' 00" Lat - N
	78° 29' 00" Lon - W

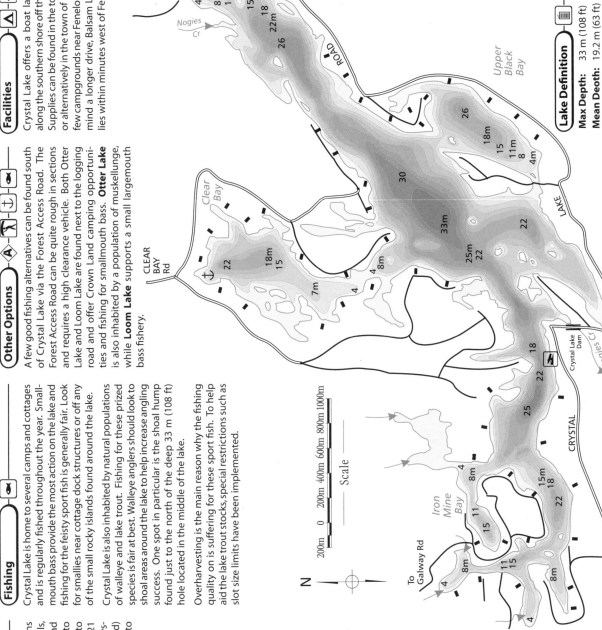

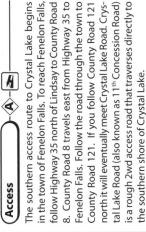

Kawarthas Key

Orillia • Crystal Lake • Bobcaygeon • Peterborough • Hiawatha • Belleville • Trenton • Tyendinaga • Kingston

Map Courtesy of Backroad Mapbooks

Dalrymple Lake

Access

Located east of the town of Orillia, Dalrymple Lake is a developed lake that can be accessed from several areas. To reach the lake, follow Highway 12 east from Orillia to County Road 46 (Lake Dalrymple Road). Head northeast along the county road eventually meeting County Road 6, which leads to Dalrymple Lake.

Other Options

In the nearby area, there are several other lakes that are easily accessible and offer angling opportunities similar or even better than Dalrymple Lake. **Young Lake** to the north is a smaller fishing lake, whereas **Lake Couchiching** to the west is a much larger lake and is part of the Trent Severn waterway. To the north of Dalrymple Lake past Young Lake the terrain begins to change to more rolling hills and is home to hundreds of fishing lakes to be explored.

Fishing

Due mainly to the easy access and close proximity to the urban development of Toronto, Dalrymple Lake is a heavily fished lake. The lake was once home to a quality fishery, although with the surrounding development the fishing quality has decreased significantly. Smallmouth and largemouth bass are the two most productive sport fish, while angling success for walleye and northern pike is very slow at times. Similar to most other Kawartha Lakes, muskellunge once inhabited Dalrymple Lake. With the past introduction of northern pike, muskellunge are now thought to be near extinction. There are also rumours of tiger pike, the northern pike, muskellunge hybrid in Dalrymple, although this report has never been officially verified.

Dalrymple Lake is divided into two halves by County Road 6. Upper Dalrymple Lake is actually the southern portion, while Lower Dalrymple Lake is the northern half of the lake. Upper Dalrymple is very shallow and almost swamp-like in several areas and fishing is often slow. Lower Dalrymple Lake has definitive weed lines that can be easily located. Fishing along these weed lines by trolling or jigging can produce results for all sport fish species.

Facilities

There are four established boat launch areas located on Dalrymple Lake, with three of the launches found in the northern end. Along with the boat launches, there are two tent and trailer parks found along the shoreline of Lower Dalrymple Lake (northern end). Roofed accommodations can be found in the town of Orillia to the west.

Lake Definition

Mean Depth: 7 m (23 ft)
Max Depth: 9 m (29.5 ft)
Way Point: 44° 38' 00" Lat - N
79° 07' 00" Lon - W

Kawarthas Key

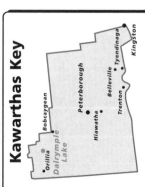

Map Courtesy of Backroad Mapbooks

(Map)

Lower Dalrymple Lake

Upper Dalrymple Lake

McCrackens Beach

Avery Point

Herring Island

rocks

To Head Lake

Lake Dalrymple

To Hwy 35

Dalrymple

To Canal Lake

Campbells Beach

Sylvan Glen Beach

Lakeview Beach

To Hwy 48

9th CONC Rd
8th CONC Rd
7th CONC Rd

To Hwy 169

AVERY ROAD
McNABB ROAD
DAY ROAD
KIRKFIELD ROAD

To County Rd 45

To Hwy 12

Scale
500m 0 1km 2km 3km

N

Dickey Lake

Kawarthas Key

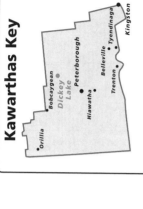

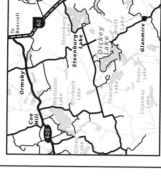

Map Courtesy of Backroad Mapbooks

Access

Dickey Lake is located in a more remote region of the Kawarthas in the expanse of land found between Highway 28 and Highway 62. The easiest way to reach the lake is to travel north along Highway 62 and turn west onto Steenburg Lake Road North. Along Steenburg Lake Road North, you will pass Steenburg Lake then the small settlement of Murphy Corners before reaching Dickey Lake. Look for signs off Steenburg Lake Road North marking the access road to Dickey Lake. There is a rough boat launch and parking area along the north shore.

Other Options

Freen Lake and Lake of Islands are very close by. Lake of Islands is accessible by boat from the southern end of **Dickey Lake,** while **Freen Lake** is accessible by a rough portage from Lake of Islands. Both lakes offer angling opportunities for largemouth and smallmouth bass.

Fishing

There are a number of cottages and camps along the shore of Dickey Lake. However, the lake can be a peaceful lake to fish even during the busiest times of the summer cottage rush. Fishing in the lake is best for smallmouth and largemouth bass, which can be found throughout the lake along shore structure areas. There are a few weedier parts of the lake where you can find largemouth bass, while smallmouth are often found near rocky shoreline structures. It is also recommended to try near man-made shore structures such as docks. Bass can sometimes be found hiding in the shade of the wharf.

A natural population of lake trout also inhabits the lake but fishing is often slow. Ice fishing in the winter is a productive method for lake trout, while trolling silver spoons in spring can also provide results. To help protect lake trout stocks, there are special ice fishing and slot size restrictions in place. As a fragile species, it is recommended to practice catch and release for lake trout whenever possible.

Lake Definition

Mean Depth: 18.3 m (60 ft)
Max Depth: 42.7 m (140 ft)
Way Point: 44°47'00" Lat - N
77°44'00" Lon - W

Facilities

The boat launch is the main facility found on Dickey Lake. Rustic Crown Land camping opportunities can be found south of Dickey Lake at Freen Lake, although a portage is required to access the lake. Your best bet for accommodations and supplies is either the town of Bancroft to the north or the town of Madoc to the south.

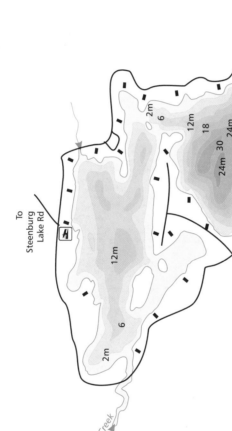

To Steenburg Lake Rd

To Old Hastings Rd

Dickey Creek

Lake of Islands

2m
6
12m
18
24m
24m
30
36m
2m
6
12m
2m
6
18
24m
30

N

Scale

200m 0 200m 400m 600m 800m 1000m

Dummer (White) Lake

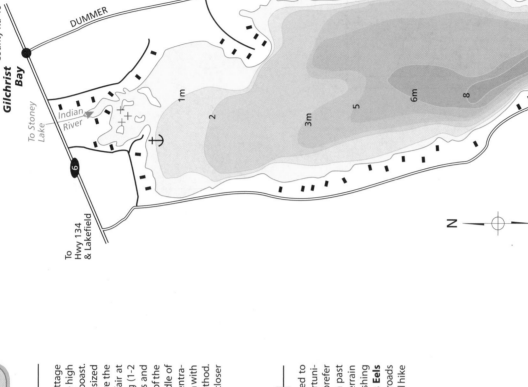

Access

Dummer Lake is located just south of the much larger Stoney Lake. To find the lakes, follow Highway 7 east from Peterborough to Highway 134. Travel north along Highway 134 to the Highway 28 junction. Look for County Road 6 (Stoney Lake Road) leading east from Highway 28. A marina on Dummer Lake is accessible off a small access road off the south side of County Road 6.

Facilities

Other than the marina, there are no facilities available on Dummer Lake. There are tent and trailer parks in the area on Stoney Lake and Buckhorn Lake near Burleigh Falls. Otherwise, roofed accommodations, such as motels, are available in the town of Lakefield or the city of Peterborough to the south.

Fishing

Dummer Lake remains a popular Kawartha cottage destination lake and anglers benefit from the high nutrient base that most of the Kawartha Lakes boast. Fishing in the lake is generally fair for nice sized smallmouth and largemouth bass. Walleye are the other main sport fish but fishing is slow to fair at times for walleye that average about 0.5-1 kg (1-2 lbs) in size. Look for walleye along weed lines and along the drop-off located in at southern end of the lake. The underwater point found in the middle of the lake is also known to hold greater concentrations of walleye at times. Trolling over this area with a worm harness can be an effective angling method. Smallmouth bass can also often be picked up closer to shore off the southern drop-off area.

Other Options

Neighbouring **Stoney Lake** is all but attached to Dummer Lake. Stoney Lake offers fishing opportunities for bass, walleye and muskellunge. If you prefer smaller lakes, by following Highway 28 north past Burleigh Falls, you will enter more rolling terrain that is home to countless lakes that offer fishing opportunities. There are many lakes, such as **Eels Lake** and **Silent Lake**, which are accessible via roads not far from Highway 28. There are also several hike or paddle-in lakes in this area.

Lake Definition

Elevation:	244 m (800 ft)
Surface Area:	711.4 ha (1,758 ac)
Perimeter:	7.7 km (4.8 mi)
Mean Depth:	4.8 m (16 ft)
Max Depth:	9.1 m (30ft)
Way Point:	44° 32'00"Lat - N
	78° 06'00" Lon - W

Kawarthas Key

Map Courtesy of Backroad Mapbooks

Fortescue Lake

Fishing

The main sport fish in Fortescue Lake is smallmouth bass. Smallmouth bass can reach good sizes in the lake and can be found mainly along shore structure. Cottage docks and rocky shoreline areas are good holding areas for smallmouth. For the larger smallies, try closer to the bottom off one of the small islands around the lake. A ways back from one of the rocky points around the lake. A crayfish imitation fly or lure can work exceptionally well on this lake. Work the crayfish along the bottom in a short jerk type fashion to entice even lethargic bass into striking.

Lake trout and muskellunge are also found in Fortescue Lake, although fishing for both species can be slow at times. Ice fishing for lakers is best along drop-offs in the western portion of the lake.

Access

The western access route to Fortescue Lake begins along County Road 45. To reach County Road 45, take Highway 35 north to the town of Norland. At Norland, you will find County Road 45 off the east side of the highway. Follow County Road 45 to the town of Kinmount where County Road 45 essentially changes to County Road 503. Travel east along County Road 503 to White Lake Road. Take White Lake Road east to the settlement of Fortescue located near the northwest shore of Fortescue Lake.

Facilities

There are no facilities available on Fortescue Lake, although supplies and other essentials are available in the towns of Kinmount or Norland. For overnight accommodation, there is a private tent and trailer park south of Norland. Alternatively, Balsam Lake Provincial Park can be reached within minutes of Norland. The park provides a number of amenities including showers and flush toilets. Call (888) ONT-PARK for reservations, as the park can be quite busy during the summer months.

Other Options

On your way to Fortescue Lake, via White Lake Road, you will pass the southern end of **Salerno Lake** approximately 2 km west of Fortescue Lake. Salerno Lake is a cottage destination lake that offers decent fishing for mainly smallmouth bass. There are reports of catches of largemouth bass and walleye and muskellunge also inhabit Salerno Lake. The larger predators are often the main sport fish sought after by anglers on the lake.

Lake Definition

Mean Depth: 15 m (49.2 ft)
Max Depth: 27.4 m (90 ft)
Way Point: 44° 50'00" Lat - N
78° 26'00" Lon - W

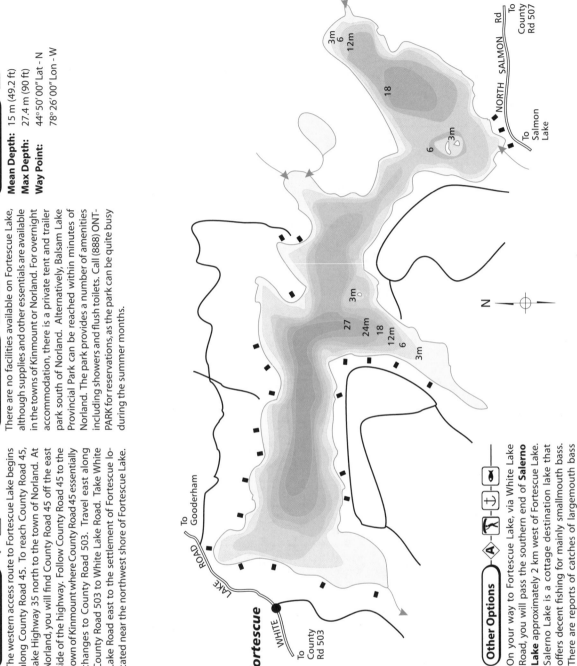

Four Mile Lake

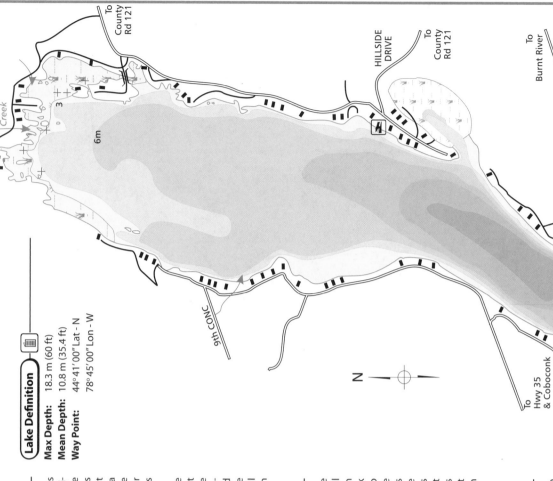

Lake Definition

Max Depth:	18.3 m (60 ft)
Mean Depth:	10.8 m (35.4 ft)
Way Point:	44°41'00" Lat - N
	78°45'00" Lon - W

Access

You will find this medium sized Kawartha Lake east of the village of Coboconk. Coboconk is easily reached via Highway 35 north of Lindsay. From Coboconk, travel east along the 7th Concession Road to Boundary Road. Follow Boundary Road south to Burnt River Road and head east. Burnt River Road travels past the south side of Four Mile Lake. To reach the boat launch, travel further west to County Road 121 and head north. Look for Hillside Drive to the west and follow this road to the western shore of the lake and the boat launch area.

Fishing

This scenic Kawartha area lake is home to numerous cottages and camps and offers fishing opportunities for smallmouth bass, largemouth bass, walleye and muskellunge. Success for bass and walleye is regarded as fair but some nice sized fish are caught every year. The northern portion of the lake is a productive area for bass, as largemouth bass utilize the weed growth in the region for cover. Top water flies and lures can create some decent action in this area, mainly at dusk.

A good area to look for walleye on Four Mile Lake is off the large shoal point located in the northwest end of the lake. A shoal is an underwater structure that naturally attracts walleye and even muskellunge on occasion. If you can also locate weed growth in the area, your chances of success are sure to increase. Trolling worm harnesses or still jigging are both effective methods for walleye on Four Mile Lake.

Other Options

The **Burnt River** lies just to the east of Four Mile Lake and is accessible by 2wd roads from several areas. Despite the fact there is good smallmouth and largemouth bass fishing, anglers often overlook the river. The bass are not overly big compared to the nearby lakes, although they can reach some impressive sizes on occasion. The river also plays a vital role as a spawning channel for both walleye and muskellunge from Cameron Lake. Both species can be found in the river in sporadic numbers just after their respective season opens. The stretches of the river from Kinmount south are your best bet for some productive fishing action. Watch for fish sanctuaries on some portions of this river.

Facilities

The small boat launch provides the main access to Four Mile Lake. You can find all the essential supplies, such as food, fuel and lodging in and around Coboconk. For the campers at heart, **Balsam Lake Provincial Park** is located west of Coboconk via County Road 48. The park is a full service park complete with showers and flush toilets. For reservations call (888) ONT-PARK.

Kawarthas Key

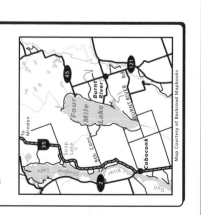

Gold Lake

Access

To find Gold Lake follow County Road 36 north of the town of Buckhorn to Flynn's Turn and head north along County Road 507. Just north of Mississauga Lake, look for Beaver Lake Road. Follow Beaver Lake Road east to the boat launch onto the north end of Gold Lake.

Facilities

Other than the boat launch located on the north end of the lake, there are no facilities available on Gold Lake. There is a private tent and trailer park available on Catchacoma Lake near the junction of County Road 507 and Beaver Lake Road, otherwise the town of Buckhorn to the south has plenty of various accommodations available. The town is also home to numerous retail operations offering supplies to help make your fishing trip in the area a success.

Fishing

Fishing in Gold Lake can be good at times for smallmouth and largemouth bass. The bass populations in the lake continue to maintain themselves despite some increased fishing pressure throughout the past decade or so. The rocky shoreline characteristic of the lake is ideal habitat for lunker smallmouth, whereas there are several quiet weedy bays around the lake that are suitable for largemouth bass. Anglers should also try near cottage docks. Both bass species can be found hunkered underneath various docks and there are a number of docks around the lake that are certainly bass worthy.

The other main sport fish species found in Gold Lake is lake trout. Lake trout once were abundant in this Kawartha Lake, although similar to a majority of the developed lakes in Ontario, the species are in rapid decline due to over fishing and lake development. Fishing for lakers in Gold Lake is currently quite slow. Gold Lake is part of the winter/spring fishing sanctuary to help the ailing lake trout stocks.

Other Options

There are several viable angling alternatives found in the immediate area. One lake in particular that can be a joy to explore is **Cold Lake**. The quieter lake is surrounded by mainly Crown Land and is only accessible via boat/canoe from Gold Lake or Cox Lake to the east. The lake offers rustic camping as well as fishing opportunities for both largemouth and smallmouth bass. Depending on water levels, a short portage may be required to access the lake from Gold Lake.

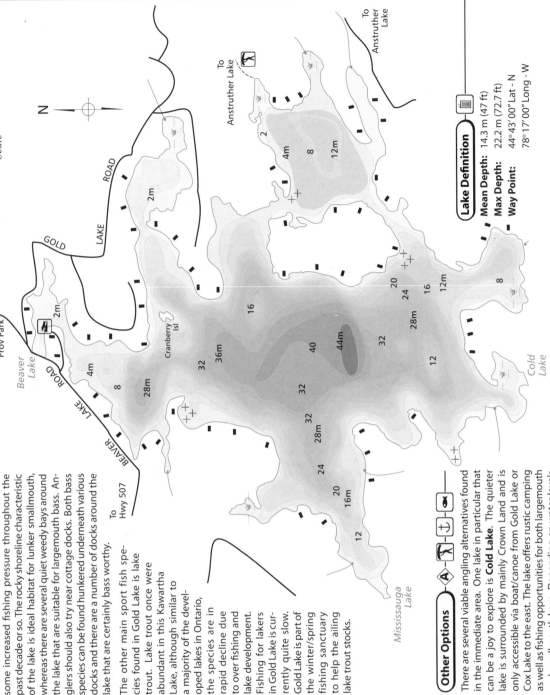

Scale

200m 0 200m 400m 600m 800m 1000m

N

To Anstruther Lake

To Anstruther Lake

To Kawartha Highlands Prov Park

Beaver Lake

To Hwy 507

Cranberry Isl

Mississauga Lake

Cold Lake

GOLD LAKE ROAD

BEAVER LAKE ROAD

Lake Definition

Mean Depth: 14.3 m (47 ft)
Max Depth: 22.2 m (72.7 ft)
Way Point: 44° 43' 00" Lat - N
78° 17' 00" Long - W

Kawarthas Key

Orillia
Bobcaygeon
Gold Lake
Peterborough
Hiawatha
Belleville
Trenton
Tyendinaga
Kingston

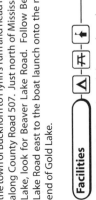

Catchacoma Lake
Sucker Lake
Anstruther Lake
Cobb Lake
Loucks Lake
Long Lake
Gold Lake
Anstruther Lake
28

Map Courtesy of Backroad Mapbooks

Head Lake

Access

You can reach Head Lake by first following Highway 35 north from Lindsay to the town of Norland. At Norland, turn west onto County Road 45. County Road 45 will lead you past the southern shore of Head Lake to two boat launch areas.

Other Options

If you continue north along Highway 35 past Norland, the geography of the area begins to change from the low lying region of the south to a more rolling hills formation characteristic of the Canadian Shield. Around the town of Minden, there are countless lakes to be explored. Some are accessible via established roads, while others can only be found via canoe.

Fishing

Head Lake has a very interesting bottom structure and is made up of many shoal humps and rock piles. Smallmouth bass often congregate around these 2-3 m (4-7 ft) humps and can be readily taken with a jig worked off the bottom. At times smallmouth can be a fickle sport fish and it may be required to slow your lure presentation down in order to entice strikes. Working the jig in an up and down fashion gives the bass time to slowly view the bait. With this type of presentation bass will usually suck the lure in on the down swing, making strikes a little more challenging to detect than normal.

A fair population of muskellunge are also found in Head Lake and the lake has developed a good reputation among musky hunters. Trolling the larger type musky lures off shoal areas in fall can provide results. Although bass anglers working spinner baits or other similar lures catch the odd musky occasionally, musky fishing is a completely different form of angling and takes plenty of experience to achieve results regularly. Some good-sized musky are caught and released in Head Lake each year.

Facilities

There are two boat launches onto Head Lake. The first launch is located near the corner of the 5th Concession Road and County Road 45, while the second launch area is found to the west via a short road just east of the junction of Suter Drive and County Road 45. There is a small picnic area at the first boat launch. Along County Road 45, you will also find two tent and trailer parks.

Alternatively, Balsam lake Provincial Park is located south of Head Lake off County Road 48 west of the town of Coboconk. **Balsam Lake Provincial Park** is a full facility park, offering various amenities such as flush toilets and showers. Call (888) ONT-PARK for reservations.

Lake Definition

Mean Depth: 4.2 m (14 ft)
Max Depth: 7 m (23 ft)
Way Point: 44° 43' 00" Lat - N
78° 56' 00" Long - W

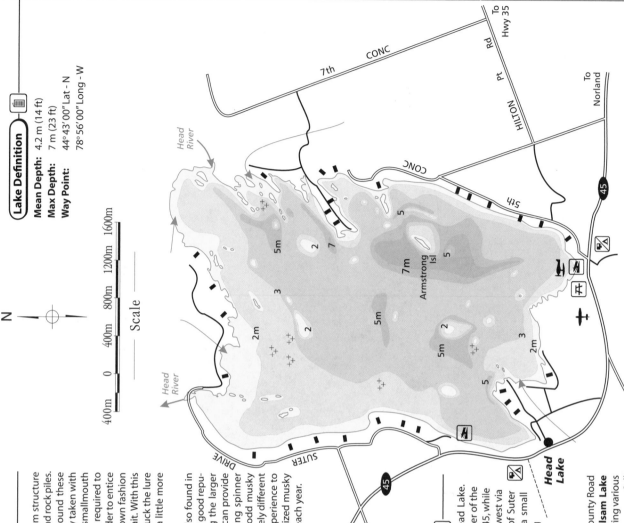

Kawarthas Key

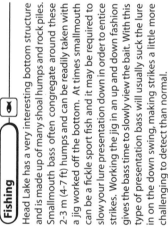

Map Courtesy of Backroad Mapbooks

Jacks Lake

Fishing

Set within a portion of the Peterborough Crown Game Preserve, this beautiful lake is riddled with dozens of small bays and islands making for prime habitat for sport fish such as bass and walleye.

Smallmouth and largemouth bass are both residents of this large lake and provide for the bulk of the angling action here. Bass average about 1 kg (2 lbs) in size, although they can be found larger on occasion. Top water action can be a lot of fun during summer evening just before the sunsets. Work a popper fly or lure along shore structure for those exciting top water strikes. Fishing in general is fair, although it can be good on occasion.

Typical of the area, despite smaller numbers of fish, walleye seem to get most of the attention on this lake. Fishing for average sized fish can be slow at times. To find more consistent fishing, it is recommended to try working off points and shoals as well as near weed lines. Walleye will cruise these areas in search of baitfish, especially as evening approaches. A good example of a decent point to try off is Hurricane Point in the southwest end of the lake.

A fair population of muskellunge is also available in Jack's Lake. Fishing for these big predators is best in the fall.

Access

Jack's Lake lies northeast of the city of Peterborough. To find the lake, follow Highway 28 north from Peterborough to the village of Apsley. Take Highway 504 to Apsley and look for Jack's Lake Road off the south side of Highway 504 just outside of town. Jack's Lake Road travels south to a boat launch found at the northwest corner of the lake.

Facilities

There is a boat launch available at the northwest corner of Jack's Lake. For supplies such as gas and groceries, the village of Apsley lies minutes to the north. Those interested in vacationing here will find numerous cottages for rent in the area, as well as the odd lodge and bed & breakfast available. Inquire locally with the Kawartha Lakes Chamber of Commerce for more information.

Other Options

While there are many smaller lakes found in the immediate area that provide fishing opportunities, two more notable destinations are Chandos Lake and Kashabog Lake. Chandos Lake lies to the north of Jack's Lake while Kashabog lie to the southeast. Both lakes offer fishing opportunities for smallmouth and largemouth bass. Chandos Lake also supports a population of lake trout and northern pike, while Kashabog Lake is home to muskellunge and walleye.

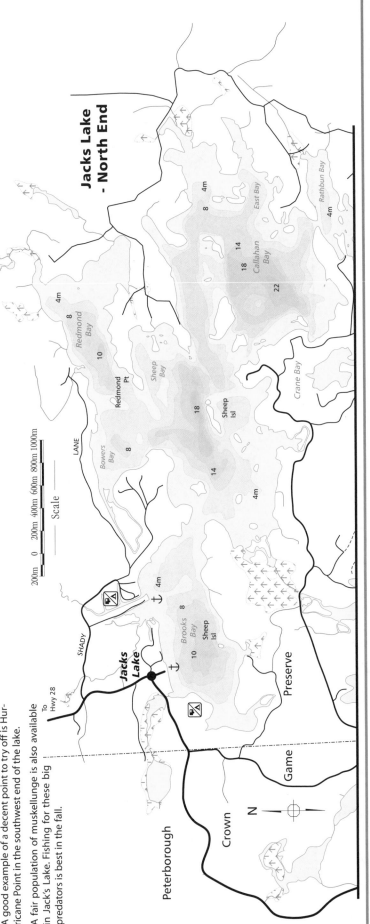

Jacks Lake - North End

Jacks Lake

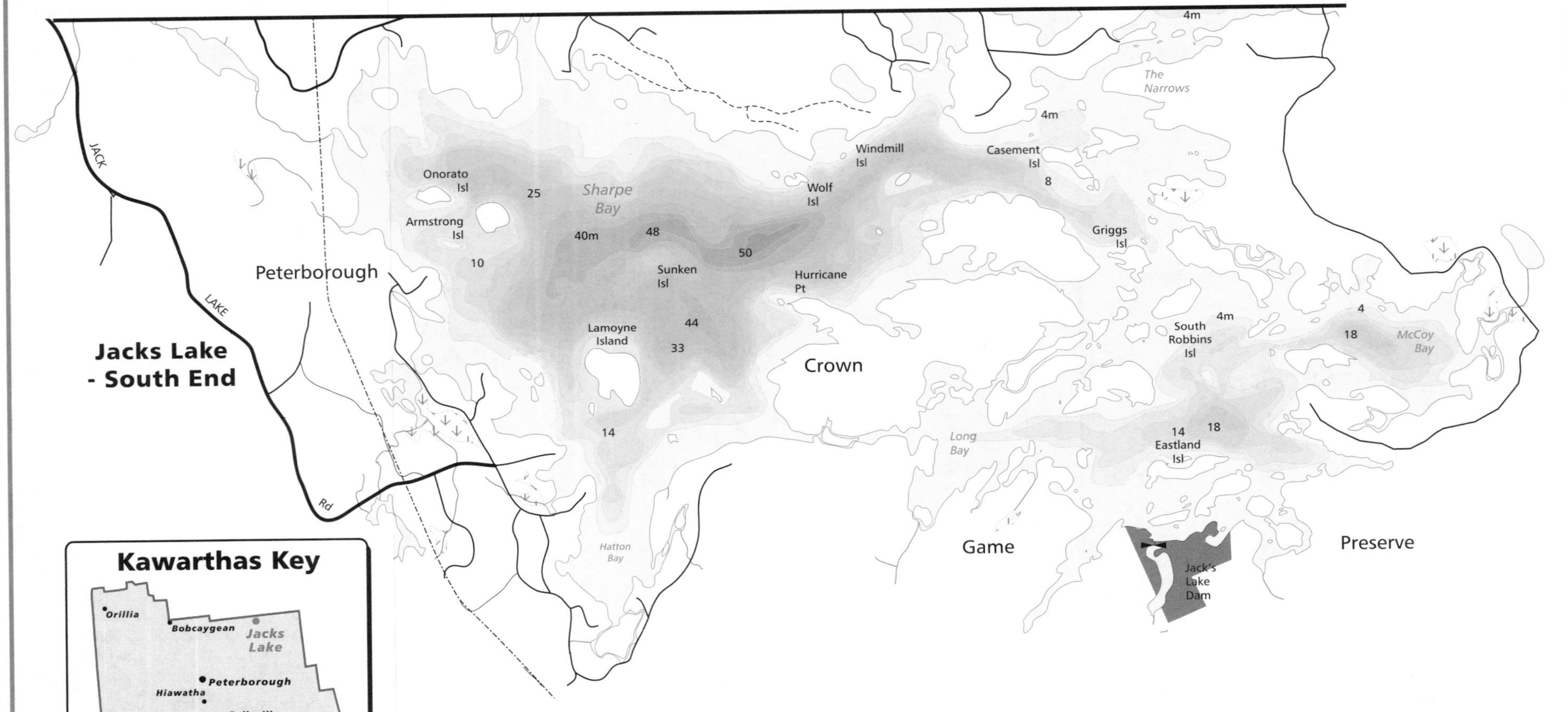

Jacks Lake - South End

McCoy Bay

4
18

4m

4m

South Robbins Isl

18
14 18
Eastland Isl

Jacks Lake Dam

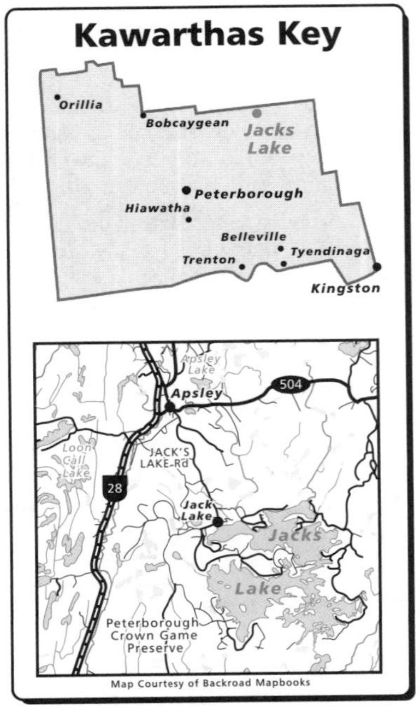

Preserve

Game

The Narrows

4m

Griggs Isl

Casement Isl

4m
8

Windmill Isl

Wolf Isl

Hurricane Pt

Long Bay

Crown

50

Sunken Isl
44
33

48

40m
Sharpe Bay

Lamoyne Island

14

Hatton Bay

25

10

Onorato Isl

Armstrong Isl

Peterborough

JACK LAKE Rd

Lake Definition

Elevation: 278 m (912 ft)
Surface Area: 1221 ha (3,013 ac)
Max Depth: 42.7 m (140 ft)
Mean Depth: 8.4 m (27.5 ft)
Way Point: 44°37'00"Lat - N
78°02'00"Lon - W

Kawarthas Key

Orillia
Bobcaygeon
Jacks Lake
Peterborough
Hiawatha
Belleville
Tyendinaga
Trenton
Kingston

504
Apsley
Jack Lake
JACK'S LAKE Rd
28
Jacks Lake
Peterborough Crown Game Preserve

Map Courtesy of Backroad Mapbooks

Julian Lake

Access

Follow Highway 28 north from Lakefield past the settlement of Burleigh Falls. Not far past Burleigh falls, you can find Julian Lake Road off the west side of the highway. Although the lake is very close to Highway 28, Julian Lake is not readily noticeable and offers some seclusion from the busy roadway.

Other Options

North of Julian Lake there are a multitude of different lakes available for fishing. There is a whole series of interconnected lakes north of **Big Cedar Lake** that are all accessible via canoe and a series of portages. These lakes offer fishing opportunities from lake trout to bass and provide real seclusion from the hustle and bustle of urban life. You can also try a few of the easier accessible lakes to the north off Highway 28, such as **Silent Lake, Eels Lake** or **Paudash Lake**. All three lakes have plenty to offer anglers.

Fishing

Smallmouth bass provide the mainstay of the sport fishery and can be found throughout the lake. A few of the more popular areas to fish are over one of the 1-3 m (2-7 ft) shoal humps that can be found in the lake. Just off the small island can also be a decent holding area for smallmouth bass. Try working a jig near the bottom off these shoals to find those lunker smallmouth. Some nice sized bass are caught in Julian Lake annually.

A population of muskellunge also inhabits the lake. The size of these large fish can be quite a sight when compared to the size of the lake. Muskellunge fishing is best in the fall when musky generally move closer to shore structure as the cool temperatures arrive. Trolling the deeper areas of the lake is recommended during the summer months.

Facilities

Near the southern end of Julian Lake there is a tent and trailer park available for overnight accommodations. Further to the west along Julian Lake Road, there is another tent and trailer park available on Big Cedar Lake. For roofed accommodation, the town of Lakefield is merely minutes away offering various motels and bed and breakfasts.

Lake Definition

Elevation:	259 m (850 ft)
Perimeter:	4.2 km (2.6 mi)
Mean Depth:	8.8 m (28.9 ft)
Max Depth:	13 m (42.6 ft)
Way Point:	44° 36' 40" Lat - N
	78° 09' 45" Lon - W

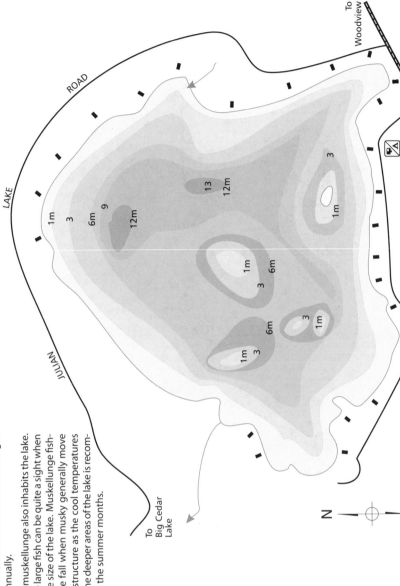

Kawarthas Key

Map Courtesy of Backroad Mapbooks

Kasshabog Lake West & East

Access

Kasshabog Lake lies to the east of Petroglyphs Provincial Park and is accessible from the east or west. From the east, the lake can be reached by following County Road 6 past Stoney Lake to West Kosh Drive. From the west, the lake can be found by following Highway 7 east to County Road 46 just outside of Havelock. County Road 46 can be followed north all the way to the lake.

Fishing

Kasshabog Lake once was home to a very productive walleye fishery, although over-harvesting has resulted in a dwindled population. Today, fishing for walleye is usually slow with occasional productive periods throughout the season.

The lake is part of the water control system for the Trent Severn Waterway and is dammed at the mouth of the North River along the southern shore. The countless bays, inlets and islands around the lake make for great bass habitat. Fishing for both smallmouth and largemouth bass is fair to good at times for some nice sized bass. There is also a small population of muskellunge resident in Kasshabog Lake.

Facilities

There are a few small marinas located on Kasshabog Lake, most notably near Stony Lake Bay. Other than the marina access points, there is a public boat launch onto MacDonald Bay on the northeast end and onto Stony Lake Bay on the southwest end.

Accommodations are available at the towns of Havelock or Norwood to the south of Kasshabog Lake. There is also a tent and trailer park to the south off County Road 6 on Stony Lake.

Other Options

Two more out of the way lakes that can provide for some productive sport fishing are **West Twin Lake** and **Sandy Lake**. These two lakes lie to the east of Kasshabog Lake and are inhabited by smallmouth bass and muskellunge. West Twin Lake also boasts a healthy population of largemouth bass. The lakes are much smaller than Kasshabog, although the fishing productivity can make them good alternate choices.

Lake Definition

Mean Depth: 13.7 m (45 ft)
Max Depth: 24.3 m (80 ft)
Way Point: 44°38'00"Lat - N
77°58'00"Long - W

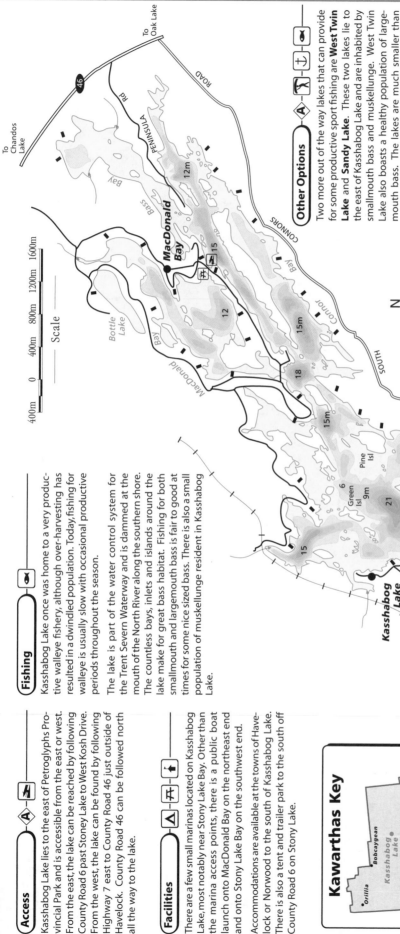

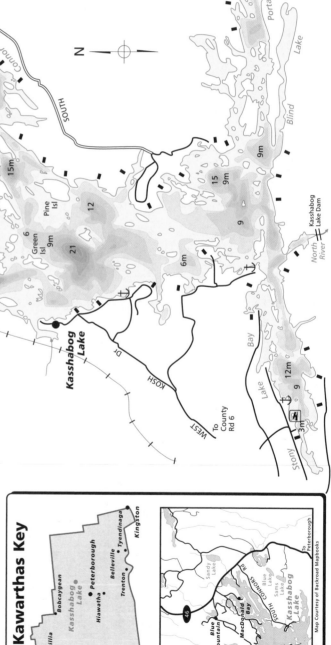

Kawarthas Key

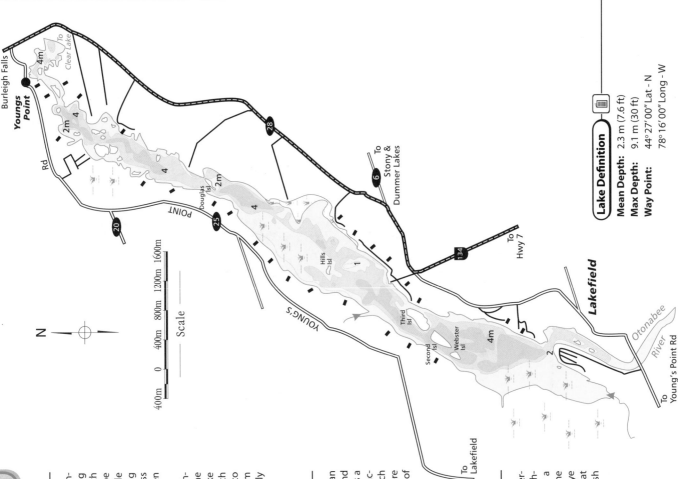

Lake Definition

Mean Depth: 2.3 m (7.6 ft)
Max Depth: 9.1 m (30 ft)
Way Point: 44° 27'00" Lat - N
78° 16'00" Long - W

Katchewanooka Lake

Access

This Trent Severn Waterway lake is the picturesque backdrop to the north portion of the town of Lakefield. The lake was created by the damming of the Otonabee River and is the first in a large chain of lakes stretching to the Georgian Bay. The main access area to the lake is from the town of Lakefield, which is found north of Peterborough and Highway 7. From Highway 7 follow Highway 134 north to where the highway turns into Highway 28. You can find a boat launch to the lake along the southern shore not far off Bridge Street (Highway 28).

Fishing

Similar to several of the Trent Severn lakes, Katchewanooka Lake is a shallow water body. Fishing in the lake is best for largemouth and smallmouth bass, as the aggressive sport fish can literally be found almost anywhere in the lake. The ample weed structure in the lake provides prime holding areas for both bass species. Many nice sized bass have been found off Second or Third Islands or even near Hills Island.

Walleye and muskellunge can be found in Katchewanooka Lake in fair numbers and are often the focus of anglers visiting the lake. Both predators like to cruise weed lines and shoal structure in search of baitfish. Trolling is a great way to cover water to help increase your success rate. For walleye, a worm harness trolled along weed beds can be particularly effective on this lake.

Facilities

Lakefield has plenty to offer visitors; including an entire downtown retail area, several restaurants and accommodations. The town is very scenic and is a fine place to spend summer holidays. The main access area to Katchewanooka Lake is the boat launch found in the town park north off Bridge Street. There is also a small marina found along the south side of the lake accessible from Lakefield.

Other Options

If you are travelling along the Trent Severn Waterway, the **Otonabee River** to the south of Katchewanooka Lake offers fishing opportunities for a variety of sport fish. The main sport fish found in the river is bass, although you can find the odd walleye and muskellunge on occasion. The river is a great spot for kids to fish since it is full of various pan fish such as rock bass, crappie and perch.

Kawarthas Key

47

Map Labels

Washago

IR 32

Floral Park

IR 32

Floral Pt

IR 32

IR 32

4m

8m

15

25m

To County Rd 45

Green Isl IR

8m

8m

30

30m

Geneva Park

To Kahshe Lake

GRASS LAKE LINE

11

44

Scarlet Park

1600m
1200m
800m
400m
Scale
400m
0
400m

N

Hawkins Corners

Cunningham Bay

Buena Vista Park

Cumberland Beach

Amigo Beach

Menoke Beach

11

To Orillia

Lake Couchiching - North End

Lake Couchiching

Access

The town of Orillia stretches along the southern shore of Lake Couchiching and is one of the main access areas to the big lake. Orillia can be reached by any number of cut-offs off Highway 11. Other main access areas to Lake Couchiching include Mariposa Beach, Washago and Wilson Point. Mariposa Beach lies along the eastern shore of the lake and is accessible via County Road 44. The Washago and Wilson Point access areas are both accessible via short local roads off the east side of Highway 11. Washago is located near the northern tip of the lake, while Wilson Point is found closer to Orillia and the southern shore.

Fishing

The two most abundant sport fish in the lake are smallmouth and largemouth bass. You can enjoy countless hours of bass fishing on this big lake. Look for smallmouth bass off any one of the islands. Largemouth tend to be found closer to shore structure near weed lines and weedy bays. Fishing for both bass species can be good at times, the key is to find the hot spots and work them well. Since there is a lot of boat traffic on this lake, bass will often be spooky and fickle. For this reason, slow your presentations down to entice more frequent strikes. Many times a jig worked slowly in an up and down fashion along weed lines will be sucked in by ambush ready bass.

The two other main sport fish in Lake Couchiching are walleye and northern pike. The sheer size of the lake makes finding hot spots quite a challenge for anglers. In the early portion of the season, walleye will generally cruise the shallows in search of easy prey, while they will move to deeper water as summer approaches. Look for those underwater shoal areas to consistently find walleye, as the predatory fish will cruise along these areas looking for baitfish. Lake Couchiching is riddled with these shoal areas; however, they vary in depth. The key is to find the depth that the walleye are most comfortable with the day you are out on the lake. Northern pike can be difficult to locate as well, although many northerns can be picked up in the weedy shallows, especially at dusk. As the cool night falls, northerns will move in from the deeper portions of the lake in search of baitfish. Trolling a spoon or rapala along weed lines at dusk can produce some big pike. Occasionally, you can also hook a big pike off the top water fly or lure at dusk.

Facilities

There are several full service lodges and resorts located along the shore of Lake Couchiching. The lake is also part of the Trent Severn Waterway and can be quite busy with boating traffic throughout the summer months. Many boaters along the Trent Severn Waterway use Lake Couchiching as a stopping point for supplies and any necessities. The many marinas found on the lake cater directly to this clientele, with some marinas providing overnight accommodation and restaurants. If you plan to stay overnight on or nearby the lake, there is plenty to choose from. There are several motels and hotels available in the area, especially near Orillia. If you prefer, there are three provincial parks found just outside of Orillia, Bass Lake, Mara and McRae Point Provincial Parks. Call (888) ONT-PARKS for reservations or more information.

Lake Definition

Mean Depth: 9.1 m (30 ft)
Max Depth: 13.6 m (44.8 ft)
Way Point: 44° 40' 00" Lat - N
79° 22' 00" Long - W

Lake Couchiching

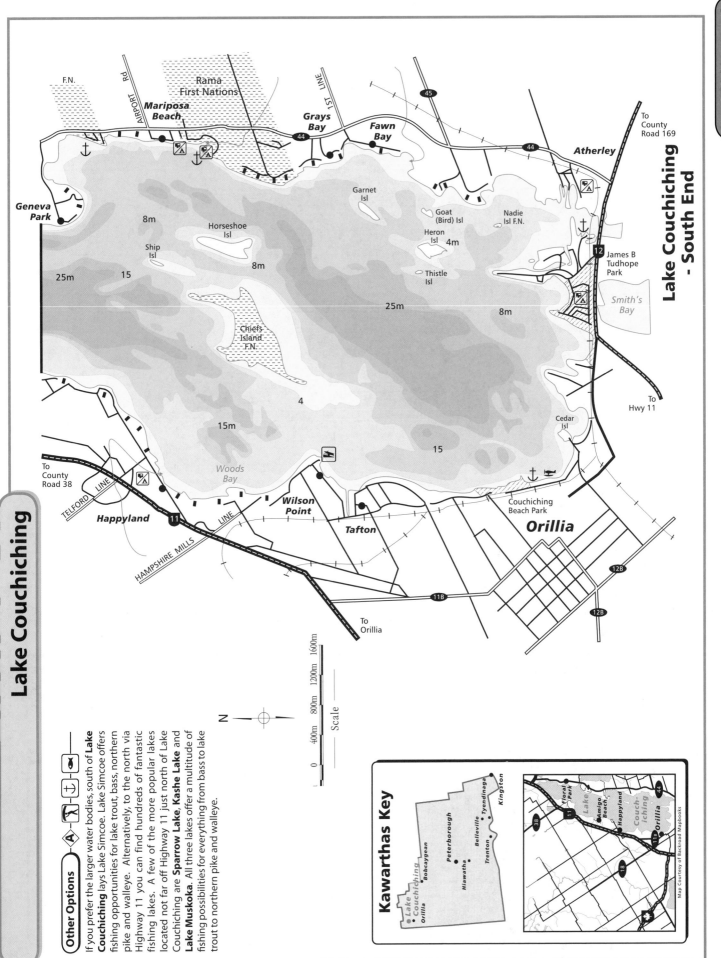

Lake Couchiching - South End

F.N.

Rama
First Nations

Mariposa
Beach

Grays
Bay

Fawn
Bay

Atherley

AIRPORT Rd

1ST LINE

45

44

44

To County
Road 169

Geneva
Park

8m

Horseshoe
Isl

Ship
Isl

Garnet
Isl

Goat
(Bird) Isl

Nadie
Isl F.N.

Heron
Isl

4m

James B
Tudhope
Park

12

Thistle
Isl

25m

15

8m

25m

8m

Smith's
Bay

Chiefs
Island
F.N.

To
Hwy 11

4

15m

Cedar
Isl

Woods
Bay

Happyland

To County
Road 38

TELFORD LINE

11

Wilson
Point

Tafton

HAMPSHIRE MILLS LINE

LINE

15

Couchiching
Beach Park

Orillia

12B

11B

12B

To
Orillia

N

Scale

0   400m 800m 1200m 1600m

Other Options

If you prefer the larger water bodies, south of **Lake Couchiching** lays Lake Simcoe. Lake Simcoe offers fishing opportunities for lake trout, bass, northern pike and walleye. Alternatively, to the north via Highway 11 you can find hundreds of fantastic fishing lakes. A few of the more popular lakes located not far off Highway 11 just north of Lake Couchiching are **Sparrow Lake, Kashe Lake** and **Lake Muskoka.** All three lakes offer a multitude of fishing possibilities for everything from bass to lake trout to northern pike and walleye.

Kawarthas Key

Lake
Couchiching
Orillia

Bobcaygeon
Peterborough
Hiawatha
Belleville
Tyendinaga
Trenton
Kingston

Floral
Park
Amigo
Beach
Happyland
Couch-
iching
Orillia

Lake St John

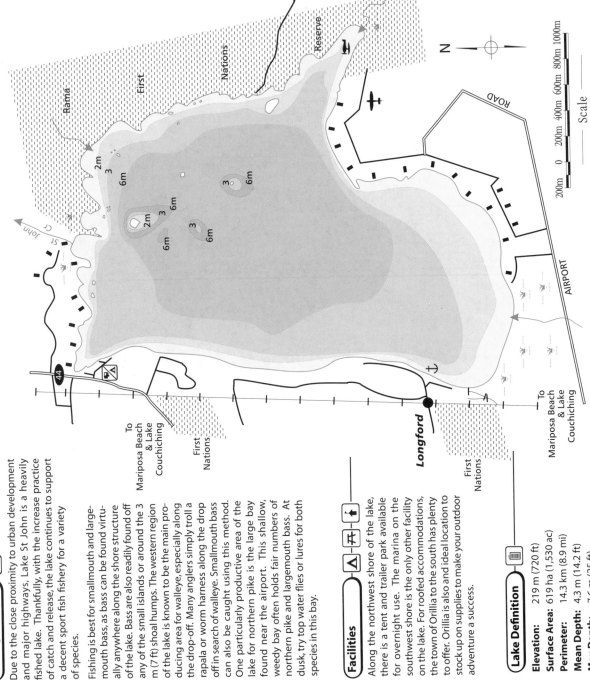

Access

Lake St John is located to the east of the much larger Lake Couchiching. From the town of Orillia, follow Highway 12 east to County Road 44. Take County Road 44 north to Lake St. John. Look for signs to the village of Langford and follow the road to the village and the marina on Lake St. John.

Other Options

Lake Couchiching is part of the Trent Severn Waterway and offers fishing opportunities for smallmouth bass, largemouth bass, northern pike and walleye. If your luck happens to be slow for the main sport fish, try working closer to shore for any one of the many panfish that can be readily caught in Lake Couchiching.

Fishing

Due to the close proximity to urban development and major highways, Lake St John is a heavily fished lake. Thankfully, with the increase practice of catch and release, the lake continues to support a decent sport fish fishery for a variety of species.

Fishing is best for smallmouth and largemouth bass, as bass can be found virtually anywhere along the shore structure of the lake. Bass are also readily found off any of the small islands or around the 3 m (7 ft) shoal humps. The western region of the lake is known to be the main producing area for walleye, especially along the drop-off. Many anglers simply troll a rapala or worm harness along the drop off in search of walleye. Smallmouth bass can also be caught using this method. One particularly productive area of the lake for northern pike is the large bay found near the airport. This shallow, weedy bay often holds fair numbers of northern pike and largemouth bass. At dusk, try top water flies or lures for both species in this bay.

Facilities

Along the northwest shore of the lake, there is a tent and trailer park available for overnight use. The marina on the southwest shore is the only other facility on the lake. For roofed accommodations, the town of Orillia to the south has plenty to offer. Orillia is also and ideal location to stock up on supplies to make your outdoor adventure a success.

Lake Definition

Elevation:	219 m (720 ft)
Surface Area:	619 ha (1,530 ac)
Perimeter:	14.3 km (8.9 mi)
Mean Depth:	4.3 m (14.2 ft)
Max Depth:	7.6 m (25 ft)
Way Point:	44°41'00"Lat - N
	79°19'00"Lon - W

Kawarthas Key

Map Courtesy of Backroad Mapbooks

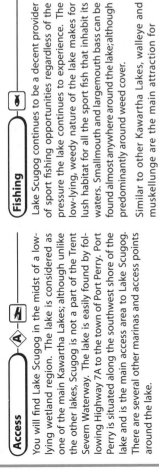

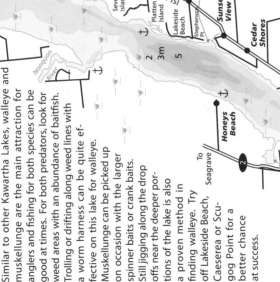

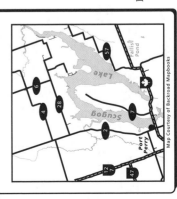

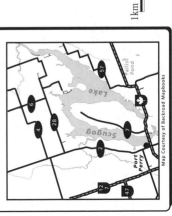

Lake Scugog

Access 🅰 〰

You will find Lake Scugog in the midst of a low-lying wetland region. The lake is considered as one of the main Kawartha Lakes; although unlike the other lakes, Scugog is not a part of the Trent Severn Waterway. The lake is easily found by following Highway 7A to the town of Port Perry. Port Perry is situated along the southwest shore of the lake and is the main access area to Lake Scugog. There are several other marinas and access points around the lake.

Other Options 🅰 🎣 ⚓ 〰

An often overlooked alternative to Lake Scugog is the **Scugog River.** The Scugog River is home to a productive sport fishery for bass, although walleye and the odd muskellunge lurk in the depths. Watch for sanctuary areas and special restrictions on the river.

Fishing 🐟

Lake Scugog continues to be a decent provider of sport fishing opportunities regardless of the pressure the lake continues to experience. The low-lying, weedy nature of the lake makes for lush habitat for all the sport fish that inhabit its waters. Smallmouth and largemouth bass can be found almost anywhere around the lake; although predominantly around weed cover.

Similar to other Kawartha Lakes, walleye and muskellunge are the main attraction for anglers and fishing for both species can be good at times. For both predators, look for weed areas with an abundance of baitfish. Trolling or drifting along weed lines with a worm harness can be quite effective on this lake for walleye. Muskellunge can be picked up on occasion with the larger spinner baits or crank baits. Still jigging along the drop offs near the deeper portions of the lake is also a proven method in finding walleye. Try off Lakeside Beach, Caesarea or Scugog Point for a better chance at success.

Facilities 🅰 🏕 ⛽

Port Perry is a scenic lakeside community offering all the essentials, such as motels, groceries and other supplies. The town is regarded as the main access area to the lake, although there are several other boat launches and marinas that can be found around the lake. One of the unique features to the lake is that it is home to a charity casino. If fishing is slow, you can always head down Island Road on Scugog Island to the casino to try your luck.

Lake Definition 📖

Mean Depth: 3.3 m (11 ft)
Max Depth: 15 m (49.2 ft)
Way Point: 44° 09' 00" Lat - N
78° 54' 00" Long - W

Scale
0   1km   2km   3km   4km   5km

1km

N

Kawarthas Key

Orillia
Bobcaygeon
Peterborough
Hiawatha
Trenton
Belleville
Tyendinaga
Kingston

Lake Scugog

Map Courtesy of Backroad Mapbooks

Lake Simcoe

Fishing

Lake Simcoe is the largest lake in the Trent Severn Waterway system. The lake has long been a part of the outdoor fun for the Metro Toronto region and is a thriving outdoor recreation playground. Although you can access this big lake from numerous areas, the main access area for the northern portion is from the Orillia area. Orillia is a scenic lakeside community that has grown substantially over the years due in part from the popularity of Lake Simcoe. There are a few boat launch areas and marinas in the town off the south side of Highway 12. Highway 12 can be easily reached by travelling north along Highway 11 from Barrie.

Lake Simcoe is one of Ontario's largest inland lakes and is a thriving outdoor recreation playground. The big lake continues to grow as an outdoor centre. The big lake is stocked annually with over 100,000 yearling lake trout, which provide for decent fishing throughout the season, especially during the winter. Trolling with downriggers is the only way to have a chance at finding them in the summer. Look for deep shoal areas for lake trout, as they tend to be attracted to these structures when holding in deeper areas. Some big lake trout can be caught in Lake Simcoe.

An often overlooked fishery on Lake Simcoe is the bass fishery. Smallmouth and largemouth bass thrive in the big lake and can grow to some record testing sizes. Look for smallmouth around rocky shoals or off islands found around the lake. Structure is the key to finding consistent success for smallmouth on this big lake. Old shipwrecks or rock piles are good areas to look. On the other hand, largemouth bass are mainly found in shallower weedier portions of the lake. A known holding area for largemouth is Cook's Bay.

Northern Pike and walleye round out the main sport fish species found in Lake Simcoe. Some big northerns can be found in this lake, while walleye success is sporadic and really depends on the area you are fishing. A good area for northern pike is Cook's Bay, as the weedy bay provides the right climate for the pike to thrive. Look for pike to cruise along weed lines, especially at dusk when they search for food. Trolling spoons or Rapalas can be effective, as can casting lures such as spinner baits. Decent walleye areas are found around the mouth of the Beaverton River or Talbot River.

In addition to all the above sport fish available, the Ministry of Natural Resources along with several other community partners began planting muskellunge in Lake Simcoe in 2005. The hope is to establish a muskellunge sport fishery to add to the current fishery that exists on the lake. For interested muskellunge hunters, it is recommended to check with local guides/outfitters or the Ministry of Natural Resources for ongoing updates on the success of the programme.

Access (north) 🚏 Ⓐ ⚡

The town of Orillia is a growing lakeside community that is home to hotels, motels and retail stores, providing all the essentials to make your fishing adventure a success. If you prefer, there are several other smaller lakeside communities and access to the shore that offer basic amenities and access to the lake. Campers will find **Mara** and **McCrae Point** Provincial Parks to be comfortable destinations for summertime fun. The parks can be busy in the summer so be sure to call ahead for reservations. Call (888) ONT-PARK.

Facilities (north) Ⓐ ⛺ 🚻

Lake Definition 🗺

Mean Depth: 8.7 m (28.8 ft)
Max Depth: 41.4 m (136 ft)
Way Point: 44° 25' 00" Lat - N
79° 20' 00" Long - W

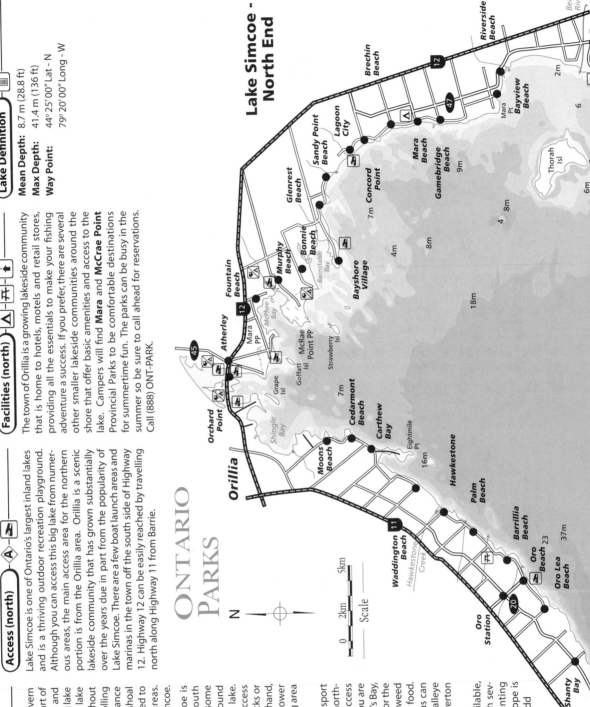

Lake Simcoe - North End

ONTARIO PARKS

N

0   2km   5km
— Scale

Lake Simcoe

Access (south)

Similar to the northern portion of this big lake, there are several areas where you can find a boat launch or marina to access this part of Lake Simcoe. The most popular area to access the lake from is the city of Barrie. Barrie lies along the beautiful shores of Kempenfelt Bay of Lake Simcoe. The city has grown substantially over the past decade or so as it has promoted itself as an outdoor lifestyle community. There are a number of different boat launching areas and marinas that can be found in and around Barrie.

Facilities (south)

Barrie is the focal point of the western portion of Lake Simcoe as it offers all the amenities of a larger city but still retains that small town feel. Hotels and retailers are readily found in the city providing the perfect base for your outdoor adventure. Other than Barrie, there are a number of alternative communities that can be found along the shores of the big lake that offer various amenities and access to the lake. For camping enthusiasts, **Sibbald Point Provincial Park** can be found along the southern shore of the lake. The park offers all the basic amenities of home, including showers and flush toilets. Call (888) ONT-PARK for campsite reservations.

Other Options

Along the Trent Severn Waterway north of Lake Simcoe, you will find **Lake Couchiching.** Lake Couhiching is accessible via the waterway or by several access roads off Highway 11 north of Orillia. The lake makes the scenic backdrop of a portion of the town of Orillia and is a boating favourite among waterway travellers. Fishing in the lake is productive for mainly smallmouth and largemouth bass, although some success can be found for walleye and northern pike.

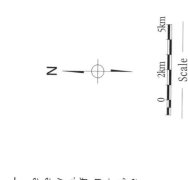

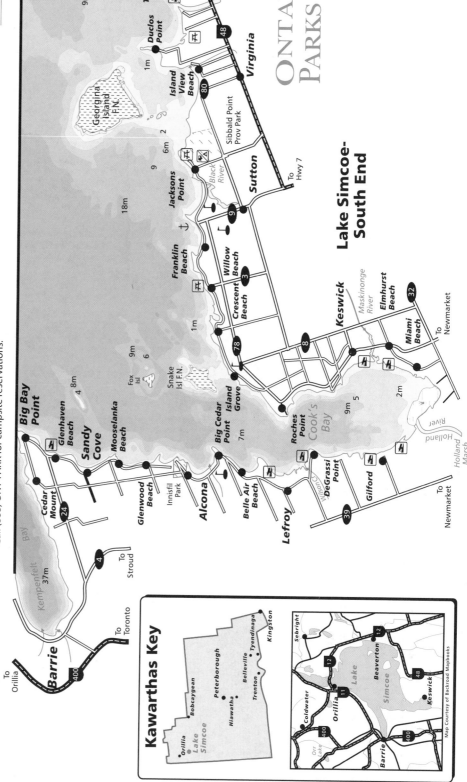

ONTARIO PARKS

Lake Simcoe-
South End

Kawarthas Key

Map Courtesy of Backroad Mapbooks

N

Scale
0 2km 5km

Lasswade Lake

Access

To reach Lasswade Lake, follow Highway 28 north from the town of Lakefield to the cut-off to County Road 504. Follow County Road 504 east past the town of Apsley to McCauley's Road. Take McCauley's Road north to the eastern shore of Lasswade Lake. You can see the access area from the road.

Other Options

The South Bay of Chandos Lake is located to the north of Lasswade Lake and can be accessed off County Road 504. Chandos Lake is a popular cottage destination lake that provides angling opportunities for smallmouth bass, largemouth bass, walleye, northern pike and lake trout.

Fishing

When you visit Lasswade Lake, you will find a few cottages on the eastern end of the lake, although the lake is not overly developed. There is a good population of smallmouth and largemouth bass in the lake and they provide for the majority of the angling action. The shallow east end is a favourite holding area for largemouth bass, while you can find largemouth in the western portion of the lake generally closer to shore. If you are looking for smallmouth bass, try off the west side of the long point or the west side of the island.

Lasswade Lake is also stocked periodically with rainbow trout. Rainbow fishing was good at times, although has decreased over the past few years, probably due to the lower number of trout that have been stocked into the lake. Fly fishing can be an exciting way to entice trout into biting. The best time of the year for rainbow is during the spring or fall periods.

Facilities

There is a rustic boat launch found on the southern shore of Lasswade Lake. Supplies can be picked up in the town of Apsley, which is located minutes to the east of the lake. For overnight accommodations, there are a few motels off Highway 28 south of Apsley. There is also a few tent and trailer parks in the area on Chandos Lake to the north and Jack Lake to the south.

Lake Definition

Mean Depth: 5 m (16.4 ft)
Max Depth: 9 m (30 ft)
Way Point: 44°41'00" Lat - N
78°45'00" Lon - W

Stocking Info

Fish Species	Number
Rainbow Trout	1400

N

Scale

100m 0 100m 200m

To South Bay on Chandos Lake

McCAULEY'S Rd

To County Rd 504

2m
3
6m
9

Kawarthas Key

Orillia
Bobcaygeon
Peterborough
Hiawatha
Lasswade Lake
Belleville
Trenton
Tyendinaga
Kingston

Glen Alda
Tallan
620
Lasswade Lake
504
Apsley Lake
Apsley
28
Scott Settlement
To Peterborough
46

Map Courtesy of Backroad Mapbooks

Limerick Lake

Access

Limerick Lake can be found by travelling east on Highway 7 to the junction with Highway 62 at the town of Madoc. Take Highway 62 north past the villages of Eldorado and Bannockburn to Limerick Lake Road. The road is well signed on the highway and should not be difficult to find. Follow Limerick Lake Road east for approximately 3 km to Martins Landing and a small marina on the southern shore of Limerick Lake.

Fishing

Nestled in the rocky rolling hills of the lower Madawaska Highlands, Limerick Lake is a scenic lake characterized by a rocky shoreline. The lake is home to several camps and cottages and the fishing quality of the lake remains fairly steady despite its development.

Fishing is best for smallmouth and largemouth bass, which can be found to 2 kg (4.5 lbs) in size on occasion. The average sized bass in Limerick Lake remains around 0.5-1 kg (1-2 lbs). Look for smallmouth bass off any of the rocky drop-off areas around the lake as well as just off the two small islands. Largemouth are primarily found in the weedier shallow bays of the lake.

The other main sport fish resident in Limerick Lake is a natural population of lake trout. As with most developed lakes in Ontario, the lake trout stocks are under extreme angling pressure. This is certainly true on Limerick Lake as recent regulation changes have been enacted to help support the ailing lake trout stocks. If you do plan to fish for lake trout, the practice of catch and release will go a long way in helping sustain this great species through the 21st Century. Special restrictions on Limerick Lake include lake trout slot sizes and only one line permitted during ice fishing season.

Other Options

A recommended angling alternative is **Mephisto Lake**, which lies just to the northeast of Limerick Lake. Mephisto Lake is accessible by water from the northeast end of Limerick Lake but a canoe may be required to navigate the channel. Alternatively, Mephisto Lake is accessible via a boat launch area along its eastern shore. The access area can be reached by taking Weslemkoon Lake Road to the Egan Creek Access Trail Road. Mephisto Lake offers fishing for smallmouth bass, largemouth bass and the occasional natural lake trout.

Lake Definition

Mean Depth: 13.7 m (45 ft)
Max Depth: 27.4 m (90 ft)
Way Point: 44°53'00" Lat - N
77°37'00" Lon - W

Facilities

Other than the marina at Martins Landing, there are no other facilities on Limerick Lake. The lake is part of a short canoe route that begins to the north on Mephisto Lake and ends to the south at a take out area off the Highway 62 crossing of the Beaver Creek.

For overnight accommodations, there is a tent and trailer park available on St. Ola Lake to the south of Limerick Lake. If you prefer, the town of Bancroft to the north is merely minutes away and has plenty to offer the outdoor traveller. The towns of Bannockburn, Eldorado and Gilmour south of Limerick Lake are each home to a general store where basic supplies can be obtained for your outing.

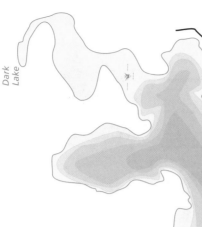

Dark Lake

2m
3
6m
9
12m
15
18m
24m
27
12m

N

Scale
400m   0   400m   800m   1200m   1600m

Caverly's Bay

Bass Creek

Martins Landing

LIMERICK LAKE Rd
To Hwy 62

Kawarthas Key

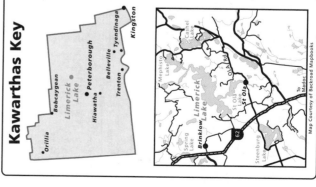

Orillia
Bobcaygeon
Limerick Lake
Peterborough
Hiawatha
Belleville
Trenton
Tyendinaga
Kingston

Cashel Lake
Mephisto Lake
Ola Rd
Limerick
St Ola
St Ola Lake
62
Brinklow
Spring Lake
To Madoc
Steenburg Lake

Map Courtesy of Backroad Mapbooks

Little Anstruther Lake

Access

Set amid the rolling hills northwest of the village of Apsley, Little Anstruther Lake is a backcountry lake that is mainly visited during the winter. There are no well established trails or roads to the lake; therefore, summer access would have to be on foot by bushwhacking. In the winter, ice anglers frequent the lake and there is often an established snowmobile trail that can be picked up from the logging road located north of the lake.

Facilities

Little Anstruther Lake is a remote lake that offers no facilities. For experienced backcountry travellers, rustic Crown Land camping is certainly possible. Basic supplies can be found in the village of Apsley to the south of the lake off the east side of Highway 28.

Fishing

Little Anstruther Lake is stocked almost annually with lake trout, which provide for productive fishing mainly in the winter through the ice. The lake trout in the lake are generally small but they can be a lot o fun to catch on a sunny winter day. Try jigging a small spoon or even a white jig at the north end of the lake closer to the Camp Creek inflow.

Both smallmouth and largemouth bass also inhabit the lake and fishing can be fair to good during the summer months. Look for lunker smallmouth off the deep drop-off found along the west side of the lake.

Other Options

Clanricarde Lake can be accessed by rough portage from Little Anstruther Lake and offers a similar rustic backcountry experience. The lake offers fishing opportunities for smallmouth bass that rarely see a lure.

Lake Definition

Mean Depth: 7.8 m (25.7 ft)
Max Depth: 18 m (59 ft)
Way Point: 44°49'00" Lat - N
78°09'00" Lon - W

Stocking Info

Fish Species	Number
Lake Trout	400

Kawarthas Key

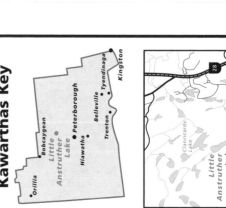

Loon Call Lake

Access

To reach Loon Call Lake, follow Highway 28 north from Lakefield past Burleigh Falls to Anstruther Lake Road. Following Anstruther Lake Road west will take you right past the boat access to Loon Call Lake. From the highway to the boat access on Loon Call Lake, it is approximately 3 km.

Facilities

Other than the boat launch located on the eastern shore of Loon Call Lake, there are no other facilities. However, the village of Apsley is merely minutes away to the east. All the basic supplies for a fantastic outing can be obtained there.

Fishing

Some cottages dot the shoreline of Loon Call Lake but the lake can be quite peaceful, even in the middle of the summer cottage rush. The lake is a long shaped lake that has rocky shoreline areas suitable for its resident smallmouth bass. Largemouth bass are also found in the lake and can usually be found closer to shore hunkered around weed structure or even cottage docks. Fishing for bass remains fair for average sized bass.

The lake is also stocked with the hybrid trout species, splake. Splake can reach good sizes in Loon Call Lake. The most productive time to try for splake is during the winter through the ice. Try jigging a spoon or even a white jig along the shoal areas beside the deeper portions of the lake.

Other Options

Fortunately, if your luck is slow on Loon Call Lake, there are plenty of fine fishing alternatives nearby. The two closest lakes are **Wolf Lake** and **Crab Lake.** Wolf Lake provides fishing for smallmouth bass and muskellunge, while Crab Lake offers fishing for smallmouth bass.

Lake Definition

Elevation:	351 m (1,150 ft)
Perimeter:	12.1 km (7.51 mi)
Mean Depth:	7.7 m (25.5 ft)
Max Depth:	16.4 m (54 ft)
Way Point:	44° 44' 00" Lat - N
	78° 09' 00" Lon - W

Stocking Info

Fish Species	Number
Splake	1,100

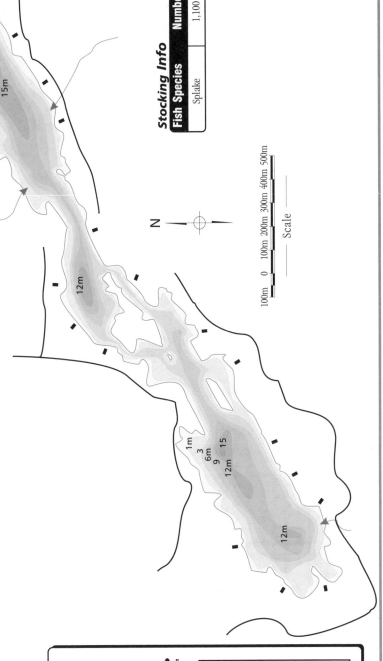

Kawarthas Key

Map Courtesy of Backroad Mapbooks

Scale

100m 0 100m 200m 300m 400m 500m

N

To Hwy 28

To Wolf Lake

ANSTRUTHER LAKE ROAD

Loon Call Lake

Lower Buckhorn (Lovesick) Lake

Access

Lower Buckhorn Lake is actually the more northern portion of the great Buckhorn Lake that is commonly known as Lovesick Lake. This section of the big lake is easily accessed from the village of Burleigh Falls. To reach Burleigh Falls, travel north along Highway 28 from the town of Lakefield. Highway 28 passes right between Lower Buckhorn Lake to the west and Stoney Lake to the east. There is a boat launch along the southeast shore of Lower Buckhorn off the west side of the highway.

Fishing

As part of the Trent-Severn Waterway, the lake experiences significant angling pressure throughout the season. However, characteristic to other Kawartha Lakes, the Buckhorn Lakes are nutrient rich due to the low-lying terrain and support a productive fishery.

Anglers will find success is often best for largemouth and smallmouth bass, as the many bays and islands make for prime bass habitat. Bass can be found almost anywhere in the lake. The key is to find weed beds and other structure where bass hold out in the greatest numbers. When fishing, one thing to take into account is that due to heavy boater traffic on the lake, bass can be quite spooky at times. If the bass are lethargic, try slower presentations such as a tube jig or crayfish imitation type lure worked off bottom.

As is common in the area, walleye are the most popular sport fish and fishing is generally fair for decent sized walleye. Deer Bay is a known holding area for these feisty predators. The area just off Black Point is also considered a decent holding area during portions of the season. The key to finding them is to locate structure such as weed lines.

Muskellunge are not as popular as walleye, although musky anglers from around the province visit the Buckhorn Lakes annually in search of big musky. Since this is a heavily fished lake, the practice of catch and release will go a long ways to help maintain the fishery.

Facilities

The focal point of the facilities for Lower Buckhorn Lake is the village of Burleigh Falls. The village and area is home to a motel and a few general stores as well as a tent and trailer park. There are also a few other tent and trailer parks that can be found along the southern shore of the lake. Two marinas, one near Davis Point and another near Victoria Springs, provide boat access and mooring as well.

Wolf Island Provincial Park protects Wolf Island and a portion of the northern shore of Lower Buckhorn Lake. The park is a day-use only park offering access to a short series of user maintained hiking trails.

Other Options

The Buckhorn Lakes lie amid a chain of Kawartha Lakes that all offer similar angling opportunities. You can further explore Buckhorn Lake (formerly Upper Buckhorn Lake) by boat to the west, while Stoney Lake lies to the east. Each of these lakes is inhabited by decent populations of bass and is home to resident muskellunge and walleye.

Lake Definition

Max Depth: 15 m (49.2 ft)
Mean Depth: 6 m (19.7 ft)
Way Point: 44°29'00"Lat - N
78°23'00"Lon - W

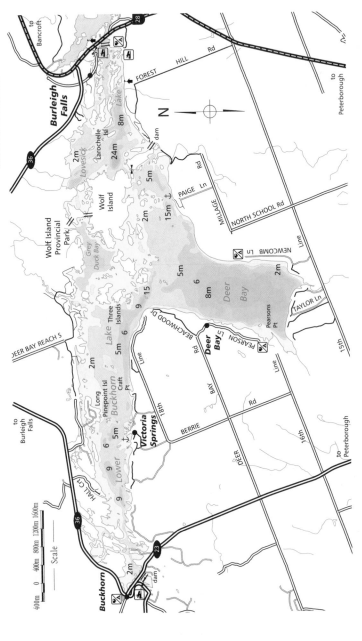

McGee Lake

Access

McGee Lake is a remote access lake that does not have any established roads or trails accessing it. The main method of access to the lake is via snowmobile during the winter. The lake is frequented by anglers during the winter so you may be able to find an established snowmobile route leading from Highway 28 to the lake.

Other Options

To the west of McGee Lake lies a fantastic chain of backcountry access lakes. The closest lakes are **Vixen** and **Shark Lakes**. The lakes can be reached by canoe and portage during the summer or by snowmobile in the winter. Vixen Lake offers fishing for smallmouth bass, while Shark Lake offers angling opportunities for smallmouth bass, largemouth bass and stocked splake.

Fishing

McGee Lake is stocked about every two years with lake trout, which provide for decent action mainly in the winter through the ice. Look for lakers along shoal areas near the deeper holes of the lake. Jigging small silver spoons can be effective but some anglers swear that white jigs are the only lure to use in the winter. The lake trout are not very big in McGee Lake but they can be a lot of fun to catch during the winter.

Lake Definition

Mean Depth: 13.7 m (44.9 ft)
Max Depth: 28.3 m (93 ft)
Way Point: 44° 38' 00" Lat - N
78° 10' 00" Lon - W

Facilities

This secluded Crown Land lake offers the opportunity for rustic Crown Land camping along its shores or on the large island. Supplies and other necessities can be found via Highway 28 in Burleigh Falls to the south or Apsley to the north.

Stocking Info

Fish Species	Number
Lake Trout	800

N

100m   0   100m   200m

Scale

Kawarthas Key

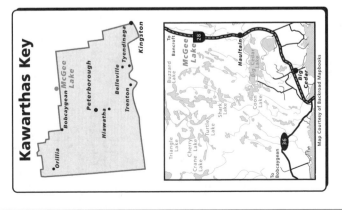

Map Courtesy of Backroad Mapbooks

Mephisto Lake

Access △A△ ⚡

Mephisto Lake is part of a series of lakes found northwest of Highway 62 and the settlement of Gilmour. From Highway 62, look for the Weslemkoon Lake Road on the east side of the highway. Travel east along this road, past Gilmour to the settlement of Gunter. The Egan Creek Access Trail/Road will soon be found heading north. Follow the access road past Cashel Lake to Mephisto Lake. There is a short access road to the boat launch area off the west side of the Egan Creek Trail/Road. Look for signs directing you to the lake.

Other Options △A△ ✕ ⊥ ✦

Cashel Lake lies to the south of Mephisto Lake and is easily accessible off the Egan Creek Access Trail/Road. There is a rough boat launch onto the lake as well a few user-maintained Crown Land campsites. Fishing in the lake is consistent for largemouth and smallmouth bass. There is also a natural population of lake trout resident in Cashel Lake. Watch for sanctuary periods and special restrictions for lake trout.

Fishing ✦

There are a few cottages on Mephisto Lake but the lake is not overly fished. Smallmouth and large-mouth bass provide the mainstay of the angling action. The rocky shoreline found around the lake coupled with a number of weedy quiet bays make for prime smallmouth and largemouth bass habitat. Look for bass along weed lines or off any one of the islands. Casting a jig or spinner towards these structured areas will often provide results for decent sized bass.

A natural population of lake trout also inhabit Mephisto Lake, although success is usually quite slow. Fishing for lakers is best through the ice in winter or by trolling in the spring. Look for lakers along the deeper portions of the lake during winter. In the spring, the uniformity of the lake temperature allows the lake trout to roam freely and they can be literally caught anywhere in the lake. If you do plan to fish for lake trout, the practice of catch and release will go a long way in maintaining these stocks. Be sure to check your regulations before heading out, as there are special restrictions on Mephisto Lake to help protect lake trout populations.

Facilities △ 𝝥 ✦

Mephisto Lake is a picturesque backcountry access lake that has a rough boat launch area on the north end of the lake. The lake is also home to a number of established Crown Land campsites. The basic campsites are accessible by boat and usually offer a rough fire pit and possibly a pit toilet. Be sure to carry out any garbage, as the sites are user maintained.

As an added bonus, Mephisto Lake is part of a short canoe route. The canoe route travels south from Mephisto Lake across Limerick Lake and St Ola Lake to Beaver Creek. The route then takes you along the Beaver Creek to Highway 62 and the take out area. The route is ideal for beginners or even for experienced trippers that are looking for an easy day or overnight trip.

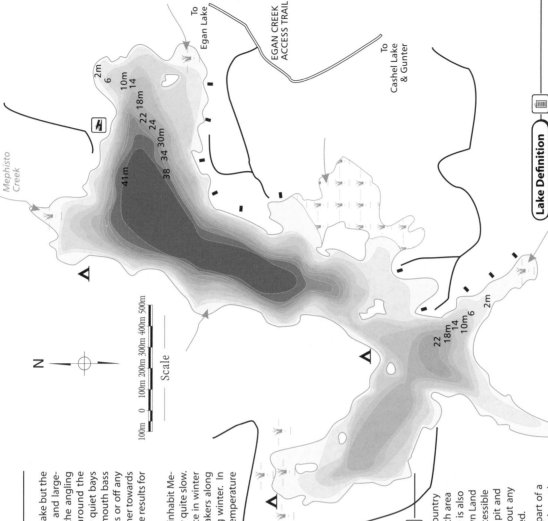

To Egan Lake

EGAN CREEK
ACCESS TRAIL

To
Cashel Lake
& Gunter

Mephisto
Creek

2m
6
10m
14
22 18m
24
30m
38 34

41m

N

100m 0 100m 200m 300m 400m 500m
— Scale —

22
18m
14
10m
6
2m

To
Limerick
Lake

Lake Definition

Elevation:	274 m (900 ft)
Perimeter:	7.65 km (4.75 mi)
Max Depth:	42 m (137.8 ft)
Mean Depth:	21.7 m (71.3 ft)
Way Point:	44°43'00" Lat - N
	77°55'00" Lon - W

Kawarthas Key

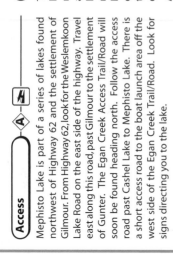

Orillia • Bobcaygeon • Peterborough • Belleville • Trenton • Hiawatha • Tyendinaga • Kingston

Mephisto Lake

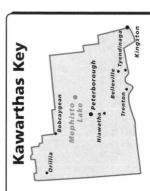

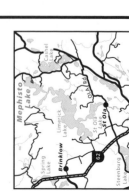

Mephisto
Lake

Cashel
Lake

OLD Rd

Spring
Lake

Limerick
Lake

St Ola
Lake

Brinklow

62

Steenburg
Lake

To
Madoc

Map Courtesy of Backroad Mapbooks

Methuen Lake

Access

Travel north along Highway 28 from the town of Lakefield to County Road 504 and the village of Apsley. Follow County Road 504 east to Lasswade and the junction with County Road 46. Take County Road 46 south and just before the road turns west, take the rough access road off the east side of the road. When following the access road, there are a number of offshoot roads leading to cottages. The last offshoot road is the route to the access on Methuen Lake. If you cross the North River, you have gone too far.

Other Options

Imp Lake is a very small out of the way lake that is stocked with splake. The lake lies north of Methuen Lake and is mainly accessed by snowmobile in the winter. Ice fishing on the lake is reportedly good at times for nice sized splake.

Fishing

A number of camps and cottages line the shore of Methuen Lake, hence the lake receives regular fishing pressure. Fishing in the lake remains slow to fair for smallmouth and largemouth bass that average 0.5-1 kg (1-2 lbs) in size. A few recommended bass spots are off the two large islands and especially near the small island found in the southern half of the lake. Around the small island, the northern portion is often much more productive than the southern side. Try a jig or even a spinner bait to entice smallmouth strikes.

Unknown to most visitors to Methuen Lake, the lake is also home to muskellunge. Muskellunge are a rare catch in the lake, although ardent musky anglers will often refute this claim.

Facilities

For day visitors, the lake offers a boat launch but not much else. Basic services and supplies can be found in the village of Apsley.

Lake Definition

Elevation: 274 m (900 ft)
Perimeter: 7.65 km (4.75 mi)
Max Depth: 14 m (64 ft)
Mean Depth: 7.1 m (23.3 ft)
Way Point: 44° 43' 00" Lat - N
77° 55' 00" Lon - W

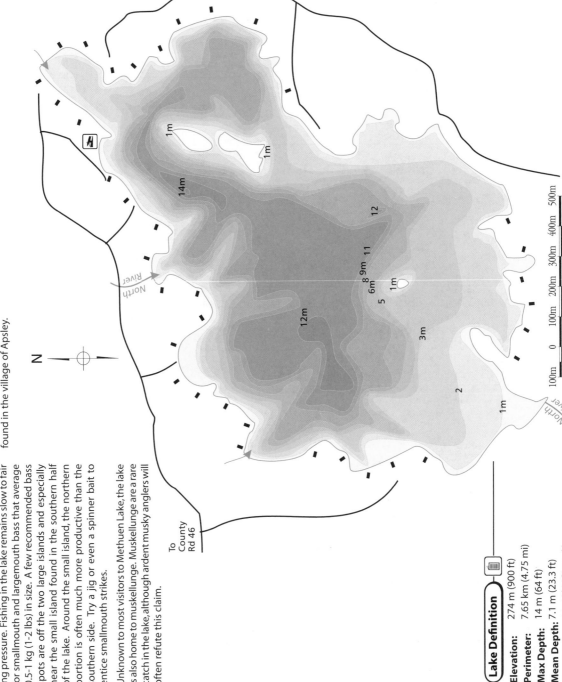

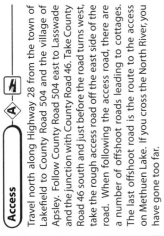

Kawarthas Key

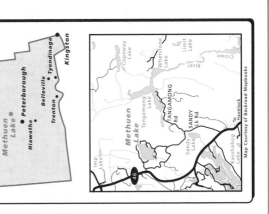

Map Courtesy of Backroad Mapbooks

Mississauga Lake

Access

Mississauga Lake is part of a series of lakes found northeast of Pigeon Lake and the town of Bobcaygeon. The lake can be reached by first travelling north along Highway 28 from the town of Lakefield to County Road 36. Take County Road 36 west through the village of Buckhorn to Flynn's Turn and the junction with County Road 507. Follow County Road 507 north all the way to Mississauga Lake.

Facilities

One of the main facilities found on Mississauga Lake is a small marina near the settlement of Mississauga Landing. There are also two other launches located along the west side of the lake. The first launch is found south of the marina via Mississauga Dam Road near the dam of the Mississauga River. The second boat launch can be found north of the marina via a dirt access road from County Road 507. Supplies and other necessities can be picked up in the town of Buckhorn.

Fishing

The rocky shoreline around this lake coupled with a number of secluded weedy bays, makes for prime bass habitat. This abundance of habitat translates into good fishing at times for both smallmouth and largemouth bass. Smallies can be found off rocky drop-offs and off any of the islands scattered around the lake. Largemouth bass love to hunker into weed growth and can be found in almost any of the many small weedy bays. One area in particular that is popular for largemouth bass is east of the southern most boat launch. The shallower, weedy area east of the island chain can hold some nice sized largemouth bass.

The other main sport fish found in Mississagua Lake is lake trout. Lake trout in this lake have continued to survive despite the continuously growing pressure on the species. Please help to maintain this species and abide to the winter/spring fishing sanctuary and practice catch and release whenever possible.

Other Options

Catchacoma Lake lies to the north of Mississauga Lake and is accessible via County Road 507. There are a few boat launches onto the large lake as well as a tent and trailer park for overnight stays. Smallmouth and largemouth bass make up the bulk of the sport fishing, although a natural population of lake trout still exists, but in small numbers.

Lake Definition

Elevation:	294 m (966 ft)
Surface Area:	588 ha (1,452 ac)
Perimeter:	28.8 km (17.9 mi)
Mean Depth:	17.7 m (58 ft)
Max Depth:	39.6 m (130 ft)
Way Point:	44° 42' 00" Lat - N
	78° 19' 00" Lon - W

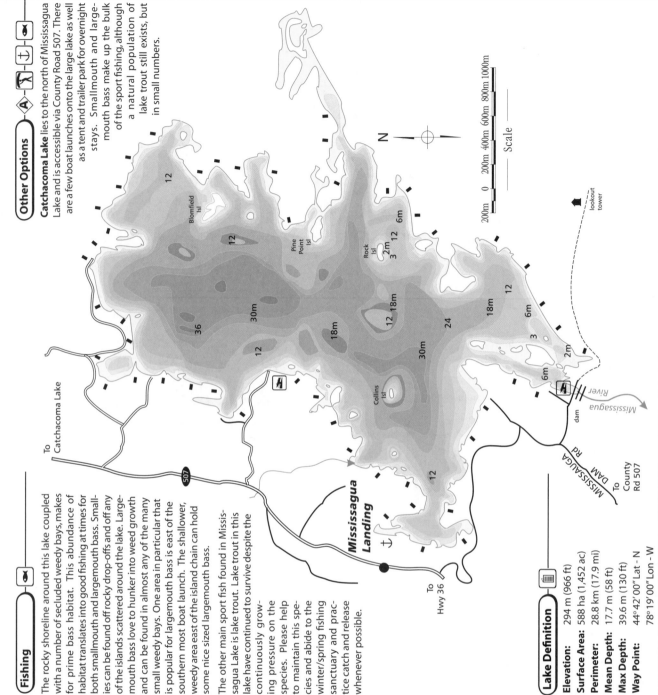

To Catchacoma Lake

507

To Hwy 36

Mississauga Landing

Blomfield Isl

12

12

36

30m

12

18m

Pine Point Isl

Rock Isl

2m

3   12

6m

12   18m

18m

12

24

30m

18m

12

6m

3

2m

6m

12

Collins Isl

N

200m 0 200m 400m 600m 800m 1000m

Scale

lookout tower

Mississauga River

dam

MISSISSAUGA DAM Rd

To County Rd 507

Kawarthas Key

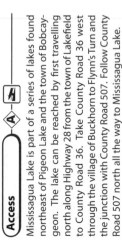

Orillia
Bobcaygeon
Peterborough
Hiawatha
Belleville
Trenton
Tyendinaga
Kingston
Mississauga Lake

To Hwy 28

Anstruther Lake
Crab Lake
Long Lake
Loucks Lake
Beaver Lake
Gold Lake
Mississauga Lake
Catchacoma Lake
507
To Bobcaygeon

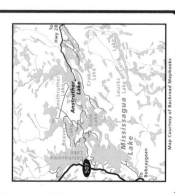

Mitchell Lake

Access

This Trent Severn Waterway lake can be found by taking Highway 12 north to County Road 48 and heading east. County Road 48 travels literally right across Mitchell Lake just east of the town of Kirkfield. An alternate route to the lake would be to follow Highway 35 north to the town of Coboconk, then travelling southwest along County Road 48.

Other Options

The two closest fishing alternatives are Canal Lake to the west and Balsam Lake to the east. Both Lakes are accessible not far from County Road 48 and are inhabited by bass, walleye and muskellunge and make for interesting fishing at times. Since Canal and Balsam Lakes are the larger cousins of Mitchell Lake, they make good nearby alternatives, especially if Mitchell Lake is crowded with boat traffic.

Fishing

As a part of the Trent Severn Waterway, Mitchell Lake can be a busy spot at times, especially during the summer. Fishing in the lake is best for smallmouth and largemouth bass, as the shallow weedy lake makes for ideal bass habitat. Since the lake receives heavy boating traffic, the bass can be finicky at times. Despite the traffic, during overcast periods and at dusk, top water lures and flies can create a lot of action. Another proven method of enticing strikes from spooky bass on Mitchell Lake is to work a jig slowly off the bottom. Lift the jig in an up and down fashion to entice covering bass to take a look. It often results in some nice catches.

The two most sought after fish species on Mitchell Lake are walleye and muskellunge. Fishing for both species can be slow at times but there are productive periods for both species. Walleye average about 1 kg (2 lbs) in size, while muskellunge are generally smaller than in the neighbouring Kawartha Lakes of the Trent Severn. Be sure to check your regulations before heading out on this lake.

Facilities

There is a public boat launch available just off County Road 48 onto the south end of the lake. Further to the west, a smaller canoe or car top access can also be found off County Road 48. The other amenities that are offered at Mitchell Lake are two small picnic areas accessible off the main road. For any supplies, Kirkfield has a few retail operations that offer all the basic necessities. For overnight accommodation, **Balsam Lake Provincial Park** is located just minutes away to the east. The park is a full service park complete with showers and flush toilets. For campsite reservations call (888) ONT-PARK.

Lake Definition

Mean Depth: 1.4 m (4.5 ft)
Max Depth: 1.8 m (6 ft)
Way Point: 44° 34' 00" Lat - N
78° 57' 00" Long - W

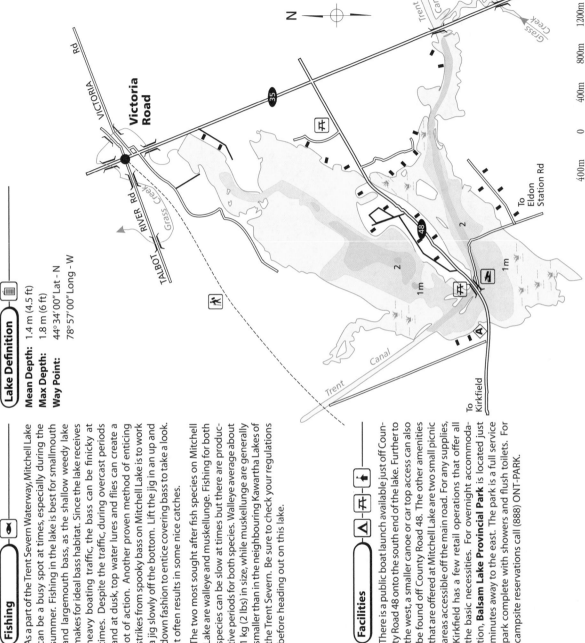

Kawarthas Key

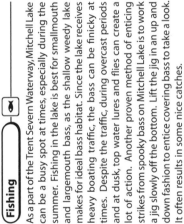

Map Courtesy of Backroad Mapbooks

Moira Lake

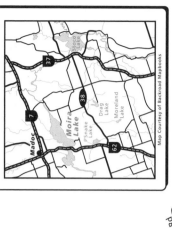

Map Courtesy of Backroad Mapbooks

Access

Located just south of the town of Madoc, Moira Lake is the main geographical feature of the area. Madoc can be reached by travelling east from Peterborough via Highway 7 or by travelling north via Highway 62 from Highway 401 at Belleville. Highway 62 crosses the western portion of Moira Lake. There are also a number of access roads that branch from the highway to the lake. A boat launch can be found off the east side of Highway 62.

Other Options

If you travel north along Highway 62 past Highway 7, you will eventually reach more hilly terrain coupled with numerous lakes for fishing. A few of the more popular lakes found north of Highway 7 are **Jordan Lake**, **Glanmire Lake** and **Steenburg Lake**. All three lakes offer fishing opportunities for largemouth and smallmouth bass.

Fishing

Originally named Hog Lake by settlers, the lake was later renamed after the Earl of Moira, Marquis of Hastings. The lake is one of many popular cottage destination lakes in the region and despite continued fishing pressure, the lake offers a quality fishery. This is due mainly to the fact that the lake sits in a low lying region rich in nutrients.

Fishing in the lake can be good at times for both smallmouth and largemouth bass. Bass average about 0.5-1 kg (1-2 lbs) and can be found much bigger on occasion. Look for bass off either Green Island or Stony Island. The far west side of the lake can also be surprisingly productive at times.

Other sport fish that can be found in the lake include walleye, northern pike and muskellunge. Fishing for walleye and pike can also be good at times, especially during dusk periods. Both predators tend to cruise along the drop-off found around the lake in search of an easy meal. These drop-off areas are often accompanied by good weed growth, which can enhance walleye and pike action. The population of muskellunge may be in slow decline due to competition with pike.

Facilities

Along with the boat launch, you can find three separate tent and trailer parks available for overnight camping on the northern shore. For supplies and other items, the town of Madoc has plenty to offer visitors, including restaurants and fast food. For roofed accommodation, various motels can be found in the area off Highway 7 or Highway 62.

Lake Definition

Elevation:	155 m (508 ft)
Perimeter:	25.2 km (15.6 mi)
Mean Depth:	3.9 m (12.8 ft)
Max. Depth:	11 m (36 ft)
Way Point:	44° 30′ 00″ Lat - N
	77° 27′ 00″ Lon - W

Scale

400m 0 400m 800m 1200m 1600m

N

Moira River

Moira River

PINEWOOD PARK Rd

Stony Isl

Green Isl

6m

6m

9m

9m

6

To Madoc

Madoc Creek

62

To White Lake

3m

6

Mud Turtle Lake

Access

This remote lake is best accessed via canoe down the Crowe River from Whetstone Lake to the north. There is an access point to the canoe route at the end of Tangamong Road, which is found not far off County Road 46 south of Lasswade. Alternatively, the lake can be reached via rough logging roads to its northeastern shore. A good map such as the Backroad Mapbook for Eastern Ontario is essential when finding such hidden lakes.

To access the logging roads, follow Highway 7 to Marmora and head north along County Road 33. Take County Road 33 to Long Swamp Road and continue north. Long Swamp Road will eventually turn into Twin Sisters Road and then Thompson Lake Road. The key is to continue travelling north. As the road gets rougher, the navigation will get even more difficult. Essentially, after you pass Thompson Lake (which is not noticeable from the road) you have to head west. There are a few different road combinations that can get you to the lake. There used to be an old access road to the southern shore of the lake, although there are rumours that parts of the road are washed out.

Fishing

Mud Turtle Lake is part of the Crowe River system and is a remote access lake. The lake is surrounded by mainly Crown Land and is a very scenic spot. Smallmouth and largemouth bass provide the bulk of the angling action, as fishing can be quite productive at times for decent sized bass. Look for smallmouth over any of the many underwater rock piles. Often a jig worked along the underwater structure will produce some fantastic fighting smallmouth. The numerous weedy bays around the lake make great habitat for largemouth bass. Top water flies and lures can be a blast on Mud Turtle Lake for largemouth.

Smaller populations of walleye and muskellunge also inhabit the lake, although fishing is generally slow to fair. Walleye and musky tend to congregate near the inflow of the Crowe River, especially in spring just after the season opens. There are also minimum length limits in place for the possession of muskellunge.

Facilities

There are no facilities at Mud Turtle Lake but rustic Crown Land camping can certainly be a pleasure. If you do intend to camp, please ensure you leave your campsite clean of any litter when you leave.

Other Options

The area around **Mud Turtle** Lake is the beginning of a vast area of wetlands. If the fishing is slow on Mud Turtle Lake a very good alternative is Oak Lake to the southwest. Oak Lake is quite easy to access as the lake can be reached via County Road 46. The lake offers fishing for smallmouth bass, largemouth bass and the odd muskellunge.

Kawarthas Key

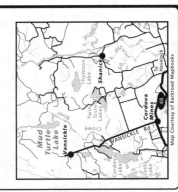

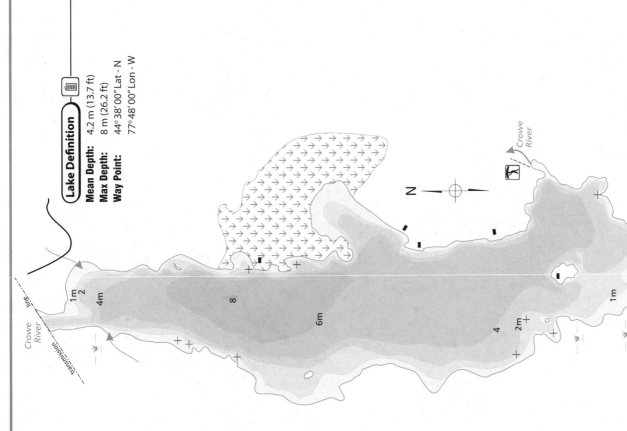

Lake Definition

Mean Depth: 4.2 m (13.7 ft)
Max Depth: 8 m (26.2 ft)
Way Point: 44° 38' 00" Lat - N
77° 48' 00" Lon - W

Nogies Lake

Access

Nogies Lake is the headwater for Nogies Creek, which runs south out of the lake through a series of small lakes eventually terminating at Pigeon Lake. From the town of Bobcaygeon, follow County Road 49 north to the 13th Concession Road (Galaway Road). Head east along the concession road until it turns into the South Salmon lake Road. Follow South Salmon Lake Road east to Ireland Road. Turn north along Ireland Road and look for the rough access road to Nogies Lake off the west side. A 4wd vehicle may be required to access the lake.

Fishing

Largemouth and smallmouth bass can be found in Nogies Lake. The shallow nature of the lake makes for ideal bass habitat. Look for weed growth closer to the shoreline to find largemouth bass. There are also numerous underwater rock piles around the lake that are great attractants for smallmouth bass. By locating these rock piles, you are sure to increase your angling success. For slower days, working a jig or other grub type lure off the bottom near structure can be effective. A slower presentation may be needed when bass are being picky.

Other Options

Nogies Lake sits in the middle of a cluster of lakes. Salmon Lake lies to the east while White Lake and Fortescue Lake can be found to the north and northeast respectively. All three lakes are accessible via established cottage roads. Bass can be found in all three lakes, while Salmon Lake and Fortescue Lake also host lake trout populations. The odd muskellunge can also be found in Fortescue Lake and White Lake.

Facilities

There is a rough car top access area along the east side of Nogies Lake that can be reached via a rough 4wd road. Basic supplies and accommodations can be found in the town of Bobcaygeon to the south.

Lake Definition

Mean Depth: 3 m (9.8 ft)
Max Depth: 6 m (19.7ft)
Way Point: 44° 38' 00" Lat - N
77° 48' 00" Lon - W

Kawarthas Key

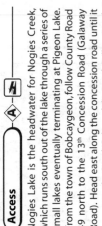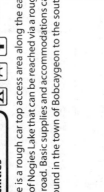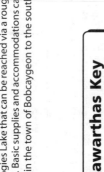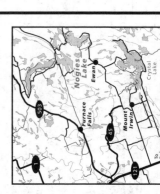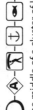

Percy Reach (Trent River)

Access

The Percy Reach is part of the Trent River found south of the town of Campbellford. The easiest way to find the Percy Reach is by boat on the Trent River system.

By land, follow County Road 30 north from Highway 401 near the town of Brighton. The county road leads to Meyersburg and near Percy Boom, which both lie on Percy Reach. Another possible access is to travel east along County Road 8 from Campbellford. About 9 km along County Road 8 there are a few access roads that branch south off. There are two tent and trailer parks that can be reached by these access roads that offer boat launches onto the Percy Reach.

Fishing

As a part of the Trent Severn Waterway, Percy Reach can be a busy place during the summer. Regardless of the boating traffic, the region continues to be a favourite area for anglers.

The main sport fish species found in the water body is largemouth bass, smallmouth bass, walleye and northern pike. Fishing for bass is generally fair for bass that average around 0.5-1 kg (1-2 lbs). Walleye and pike fishing is regarded as slow to fair but can be much better at times. The two shoal areas located near Percy Boom are known to be good holding areas of both walleye and northern pike. Try working a jig over the shoal areas, you are sure to pick up something if you have the patience. Watch for special regulations in place on Percy Reach.

Other Options

The entire **Trent Severn Waterway** offers fishing opportunities for the angler at heart, although the closest lake nearby would be **z. Seymour Lake** is part of the Trent River system that lies north of the town of Campbellford. The lake can be accessed via the Trent River or by County Road 50. Walleye, northern pike, smallmouth bass and largemouth bass are all found in Seymour Lake.

Facilities

On the Percy Reach itself, there are really no amenities available. In the nearby area there are a few tent and trailer parks that offer overnight camping. For supplies and other amenities, such as motels, the town of Campbellford has plenty to offer and is within minutes of Percy Reach.

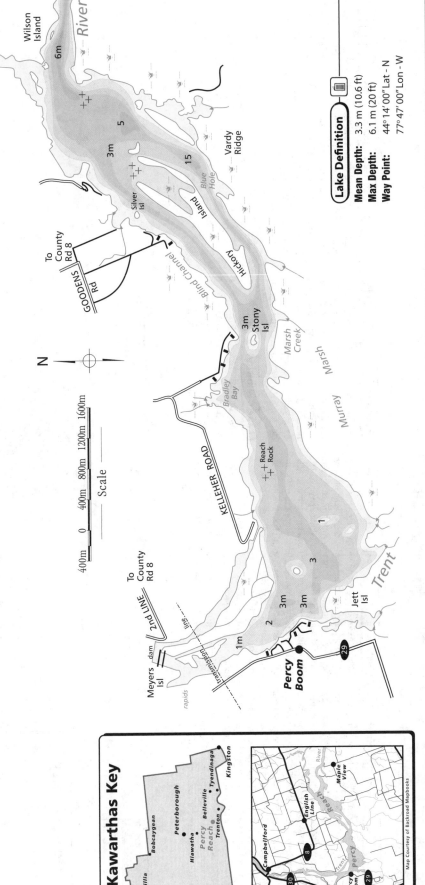

Lake Definition

Mean Depth:	3.3 m (10.6 ft)
Max Depth:	6.1 m (20 ft)
Way Point:	44°14'00" Lat - N
	77°47'00" Lon - W

Map Courtesy of Backroad Mapbooks

Picard Lake

Access 🅰 🚤

To find Picard Lake from the south, you must first reach County Road 36 and Flynn's Turn. The most direct route to County Road 36 is to take Highway 28 north from Lakefield to Burleigh Falls. County Road 36 branches west off the highway and leads past Buckhorn to County Road 507 at Flynn's Turn. Take County Road 507 north past Mississauga and Catchacoma Lakes to Baker Road. Baker Road leads west to the southern shore of Picard Lake. There was a rustic boat launch on the southern shore that is now private. However, if you continue along the rough road, it eventually veers northwest and passes the Squaw River where a canoe or small boat can be launched. Please respect private property.

Fishing 🐟

Picard Lake has been stocked in the past with rainbow trout, although fishing success for rainbows has been sporadic. Today, the most predominant sport fish found in the lake is smallmouth bass. The lake holds a good number of smallmouth and fishing is generally consistent. The shoreline of Picard Lake is conducive to smallmouth bass as the water depth drops off sharply in several areas. Look for rocky drop-off areas for lunker smallmouth holding grounds. The region around Kent Island is a typical holding area for smallmouth bass.

The third sport fish species that you can find in Picard Lake is muskellunge. Muskellunge populations are not very big, although the   a v e r - age angler can hook into a nice sized musky on occasion.

Facilities 🅰 🏕 🛶

The lack of development on Picard Lake results in a more wilderness feel to the lake. There is a very rough access area near the outflow of the Squaw River and there are Crown Land camping opportunities are available in the region. Be sure to pick up a copy of the Bancroft District Crown Land Map for details on Crown Land in the region.

Lake Definition 🖨

Mean Depth: 16.9 m (55 ft)
Max Depth: 35 m (114 ft)
Way Point: 44°47'00" Lat - N
78°23'00" Lon - W

Other Options 🅰 🏹 ⚓ 🐟

Little Clear Lake is a small lake that sits just to the west of Picard Lake and is accessible via the rough road that traverses along the western shore of Picard Lake. Little Clear Lake is stocked about every two years with brook trout, which are best fished through the ice during winter.

Kawarthas Key

Map Courtesy of Backroad Mapbooks

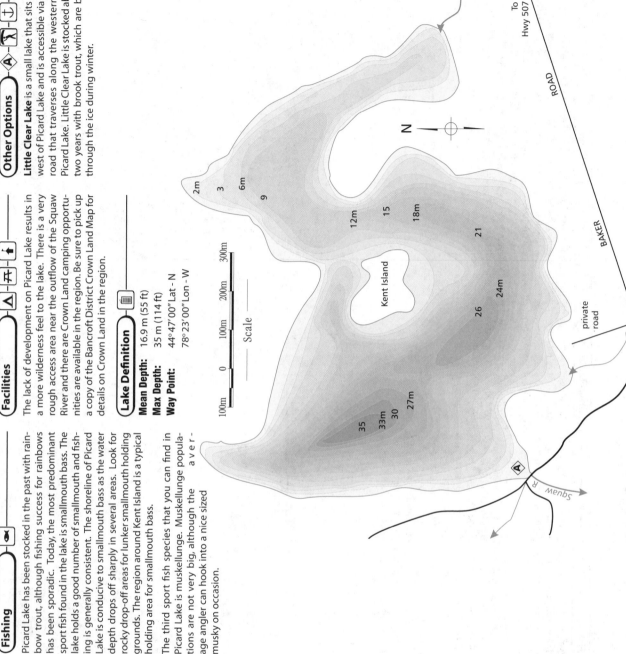

Kent Island

2m
3
6m
9
12m
15
18m
21
24m
26
27m
30
33m
35

Squaw R

private road

BAKER

ROAD

To Hwy 507

N

Scale
100m 0 100m 200m 300m

E-licence Service
for Anglers and Hunters

If you hold an Ontario Outdoors Card, you can purchase fishing and/or small game hunting licences online, for instant use.

Visit the Ontario Ministry of Natural Resources' E-licensing website at

www.outdoorscard.mnr.gov.on.ca

to purchase these selected licences online:
- 3-year sport fishing licence
- 3-year conservation fishing licence
- 3-year small game licence
- 1-year sport fishing licence
- 1-year conservation fishing licence
- 1-year small game licence

Shop Online
www.themnrstore.mnr.gov.on.ca

- Air Photos
- Maps
- Merchandise
- Outdoors Card Renewal
- Publications

The Ministry of Natural Resources

Ontario

Pigeon Lake

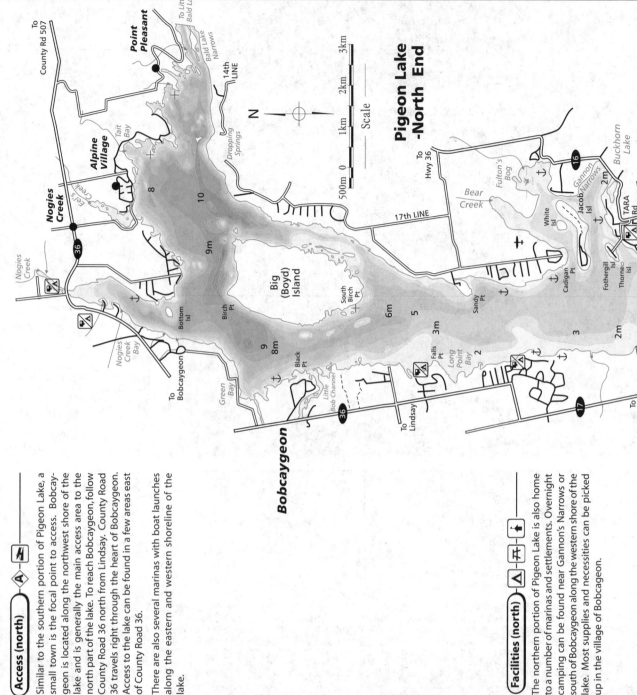

Fishing

Pigeon Lake is regarded by many as the best lake for fishing in the famous chain of Kawartha Lakes. The large lake is home to abundant weed growth and other structure; such as rocky shoal areas, making for prime habitat for a variety of sport fish species.

The most sought after sport fish in the lake is walleye. Fishing for walleye can be good at times for nice sized fish that can be found along weed lines and off shoal areas. The shoals off the southwest side of Big Island area known to be decent holding areas for a number of sport fishing including walleye. Gannon's Narrows is another hot spot for walleye.

Largemouth and smallmouth bass create the most action on Pigeon Lake. The heavy weed growth in the southern portion of Pigeon Lake offers good habitat for both bass species, especially largemouth bass. For smallmouth, look for underwater rock piles or try off rocky island and shore areas. Smallmouth will also hold under other structure types, such as cottage docks or launching areas. All the typical bass lures can be effective on Pigeon Lake. For heavy weeds, try working a tube jig or a weedless spinner through the growth. These heavy cover areas are often the best holding areas for lunker bass.

The largest sport fish in Pigeon Lake is the muskellunge. Angling success for musky is generally fair but success is often best later in the season. Look for musky around weed areas during overcast periods or at dusk when muskellunge like to cruise into these areas in search of baitfish. Larger plugs and lures are the preferred choice of experienced musky hunters, although walleye and bass presentations can fool some musky.

Lake Definition

Mean Depth: 6.1 m (20.2 ft)
Max Depth: 13.1 m (43 ft)
Way Point: 44° 27' 00" Lat - N
78° 30' 00" Long - W

Access (north)

Similar to the southern portion of Pigeon Lake, a small town is the focal point to access. Bobcaygeon is located along the northwest shore of the lake and is generally the main access area to the north part of the lake. To reach Bobcaygeon, follow County Road 36 north from Lindsay. County Road 36 travels right through the heart of Bobcaygeon. Access to the lake can be found in a few areas east of County Road 36.

There are also several marinas with boat launches along the eastern and western shoreline of the lake.

Facilities (north)

The northern portion of Pigeon Lake is also home to a number of marinas and settlements. Overnight camping can be found near Gannon's Narrows or south of Bobcaygeon along the western shore of the lake. Most supplies and necessities can be picked up in the village of Bobcaygeon.

Pigeon Lake

Access (south) 🄰 🛣

Pigeon Lake lies in the heart of the famous Kawartha Lake's chain. The lake is part of the Trent Severn Waterway and is one of the larger lakes in the system. The main access to the southern portion of Pigeon Lake is via the town of Omemee. Omemee can be reached by simply following Highway 7 east from Lindsay or west from Peterborough. There is a boat access area in the town found north off Highway 7, look for the signs. There are also several marinas with boat launches along the eastern and western shoreline of the lake.

Facilities (south) 🄰 🛆 🍽 ⛟

The southern end of Pigeon Lake is a long stretch from the Gannon's Narrows to the town of Omemee. Along the east and west sides of this part of the lake there are a number of full service marina's available. A favourite boat launch area of anglers is the access found in Omemee. For camping enthusiasts, there are also two tent and trailer parks as well as the popular **Emily Provincial Park** located just north of Omemee along the shoreline. Most supplies can be found in the town of Omemee.

Other Options 🄰 🚴 ⚓ 🐟

Any of the nearby Trent Severn Lakes are good alternatives to Pigeon Lake. For a little change from the larger Kawartha Lakes, try venturing north to a few of the more out of the way water bodies. **Bass Lake** offers a little more seclusion and provides fishing opportunities for largemouth bass, smallmouth bass, the odd walleye and muskellunge.

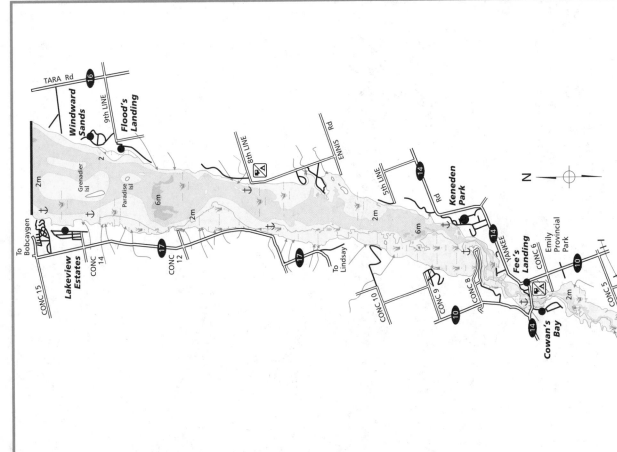

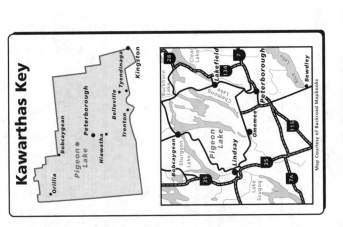

Kawarthas Key

Map Courtesy of Backroad Mapbooks

Rice Lake

Fishing

Rice Lake is one of the busiest of the Kawartha Lakes due to its proximity to urban development and Highway 401. Although the lake receives significant angling pressure, fishing remains consistent. Success is best for largemouth and smallmouth bass as there is plenty of weed cover for bass to flourish in. The shallow nature of the lake has created an endless array of shoals and weed beds, all prime areas for holding bass. The western end of the lake is very shallow and is an excellent place to find largemouth bass. Another popular fishing spot for bass seekers is the sunken railway bed found around the middle of the lake.

The prized walleye fishing is the main attraction of anglers to the lake, although muskellunge and northern pike also road the lake. In general, walleye can be found along weed beds and especially around shoal humps around the lake. The key is to find that anomaly in the lake bottom that will attract baitfish. A known holding area for walleye is around the mouth of the Otonabee River. Musky fishing is usually slow, although experienced anglers can have some regular success on the lake, while northern pike are usually picked up when searching for walleye or musky.

A big and growing attraction to Rice Lake is its panfish fishery. In the spring, you will find literally dozens of people in Bewdley, Hastings and other areas fishing from shore for crappies and other panfish. The preferred fishing method is the good ole worm and float, although the odd anglers used small jigs and even flies to entice strikes.

As a heavily fished lake, it is highly recommended to practice catch and release for all your sport fish caught in Rice Lake. The lake has suffered a bit over the past decade primarily due to over harvesting.

Access (west)

The West End of the lake has a few different access areas along its northern and the southern shore that can be picked up off County Road 28 north of the town of Port Hope. County Road 2 can be picked up near Bailieboro and travels along the north shore of the big lake. Near Bewdley, County Road 9 branches east from County Road 28 and runs along the south side of the lake. Both Gores Landing and Bewdley offer boat launch facilities near the southwest end of the lake.

Facilities (west)

The West End of Rice Lake is home to a few different marinas, the odd lodge and the village of Bewdley. Home to a couple restaurants and a general store, the town also provides ample parking near the boat launch. The Rice Lake Conservation Area is a day-use only area that can be accessed via County Road 9. The conservation area protects a vital portion of valuable wetland habitat and is a good spot for nature viewing.

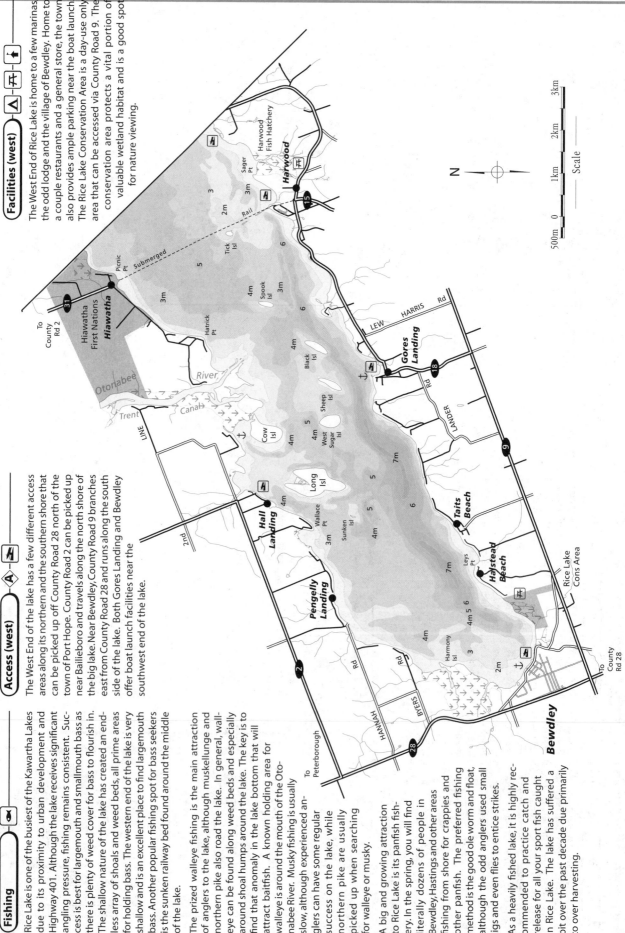

Rice Lake

Access (east)

This man-made lake is the first in the chain of Kawartha Lakes that stretches west towards Lake Simcoe. Although there are access areas at a few of the small settlements along the southern shore of the lake, the main launching area is from the town of Hastings. Hastings lies along the Trent River and provides easy access to the Trent Severn Waterway and Rice Lake to the west. The town can be found by following County Road 45 north from Highway 401 near Cobourg or by travelling south along the same county road from Highway 7 east of Peterborough. Once in town, look for signs to the boat launch area.

Other Options

The two main fishing alternatives to Rice Lake are the **Trent River** and the **Otonabee River.** Both river systems are part of the Trent Severn Waterway and provide fishing opportunities for bass, muskellunge and the odd walleye. The Otonabee flows into the north part of Rice Lake, while the Trent River flows out of its eastern end.

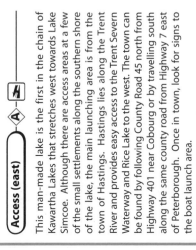

Kawarthas Key

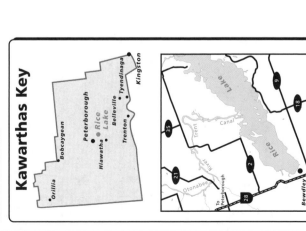

Map Courtesy of Backroad Mapbooks

Facilities (east)

The town of Hastings offers all the amenities as any small town, such as a grocery and other retailers. There is the odd cottage rental available around the lake, as well as a private tent and trailer park south of the village of Keene along the northern shore.

Lake Definition

Mean Depth: 2.3 m (7.6 ft)
Max Depth: 7 m (23 ft)
Way Point: 44°12'00" Lat - N
78°10'00" Long - W

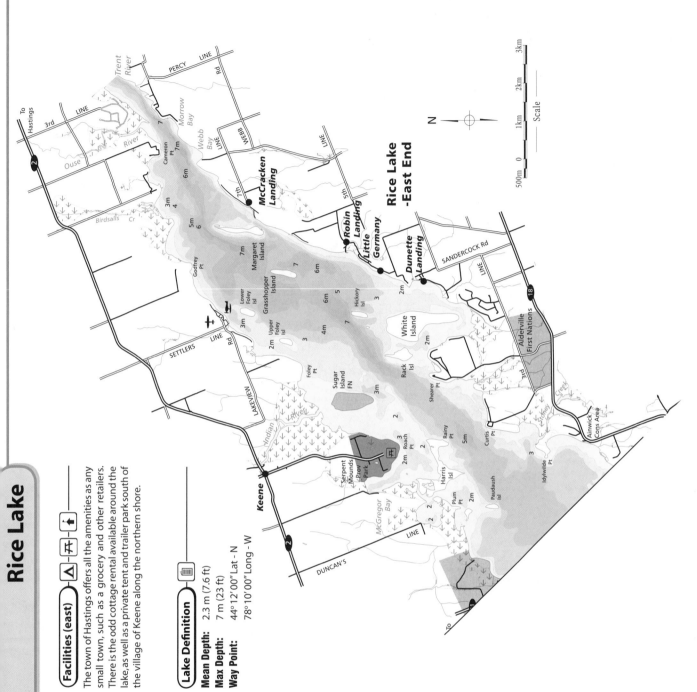

Rice Lake
-East End

Robinson Lake

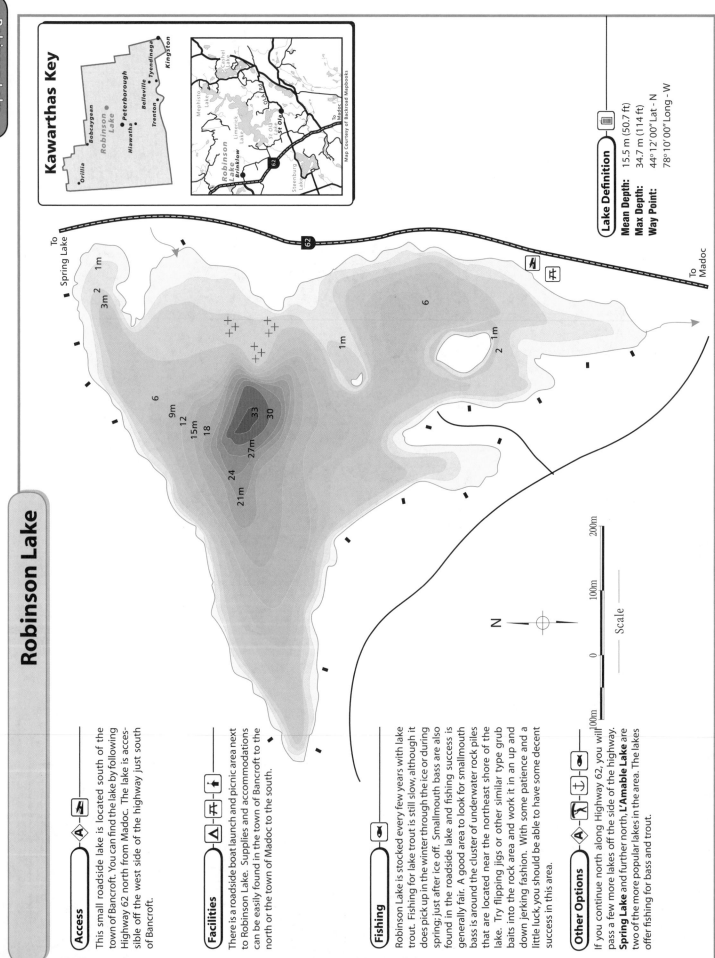

Kawarthas Key

Orillia
Bobcaygeon
Robinson Lake
Peterborough
Hiawatha
Belleville
Trenton
Tyendinaga
Kingston

Mephisto
Castel Lake
Old Rd
St Ola
Limerick Lake
St Ola
Robinson Lake
Brinklow
62
Steenburg Lake
To Madoc

Map Courtesy of Backroad Mapbooks

Access

This small roadside lake is located south of the town of Bancroft. You can find the lake by following Highway 62 north from Madoc. The lake is accessible off the west side of the highway just south of Bancroft.

Facilities

There is a roadside boat launch and picnic area next to Robinson Lake. Supplies and accommodations can be easily found in the town of Bancroft to the north or the town of Madoc to the south.

Fishing

Robinson Lake is stocked every few years with lake trout. Fishing for lake trout is still slow, although it does pick up in the winter through the ice or during spring; just after ice off. Smallmouth bass are also found in the roadside lake and fishing success is generally fair. A good area to look for smallmouth bass is around the cluster of underwater rock piles that are located near the northeast shore of the lake. Try flipping jigs or other similar type grub baits into the rock area and work it in an up and down jerking fashion. With some patience and a little luck, you should be able to have some decent success in this area.

Other Options

If you continue north along Highway 62, you will pass a few more lakes off the side of the highway. **Spring Lake** and further north, **L'Amable Lake** are two of the more popular lakes in the area. The lakes offer fishing for bass and trout.

Lake Definition

Mean Depth: 15.5 m (50.7 ft)
Max Depth: 34.7 m (114 ft)
Way Point: 44°12'00"Lat - N
78°10'00" Long - W

To Spring Lake

To Madoc

62

1m
2
3m
6
1m
2 1m
6
9m
12
15m
18
27m
33
30
24
21m

N

Scale
0   100m   200m

Round Lake

Access △ 🔧

North of the town of Havelock, you can find Round Lake by travelling north off Highway 7 along County Road 46. County Road 46 traverses past the west side of the lake. The main access is via the tent and trailer park located at the end of a short road that branches off the east side of County Road 46.

Facilities △ 🎣 📍

The only amenity available on Round Lake is the tent and trailer park located along the western shore. For supplies or other trip necessities, the town of Havelock has plenty to offer. Roofed accommodation can be found just outside of town along Highway 7 in either direction.

Fishing 🐟

As a popular summer destination lake, Round Lake receives significant angling pressure throughout the year; however, the fishing remains fairly steady. The two most abundant sport fish found in the lake are smallmouth and largemouth bass but walleye are the fish of choice of anglers in the area.

Bass can be found throughout the lake and make up the bulk of the fishing activity. A few of the better areas for largemouth bass are around the inflow and outflow areas of the North River. The weedy habitat makes for prime largemouth cover and often largemouth can be caught off the top with popper flies and lures. Smallmouth bass habitat is also in abundance in Round Lake as there are several underwater rock piles around the lake that are favourite holding areas of smallmouth. The 2 m (4.5 ft) shoal hump found in the middle of the lake is worth a try. Work a jig over the hump in an up and down fashion, you may be pleasantly surprised.

Walleye are the most prized sport fish found in Round Lake and they receive heavy fishing pressure throughout the season. Walleye fishing is usually slow, although at times it can pick up. In the early part of the season, look for walleye around the inflow and outflow areas of the North River. As the season progresses, walleye will seek the deeper portions of the lake, but they can be regularly found cruising the shoal areas. The few 5 m (11 ft) shoal humps is a mid season holding area for walleye.

Other Options △ 🎣 📍 🐟

Belmont Lake to the east of Round Lake is the closest angling alternative and is a fine choice. Belmont Lake is accessible via County Road 48 and offers fishing opportunities for smallmouth bass, largemouth bass, walleye and northern pike. Bass fishing is often the most productive sport fishery on the lake.

Lake Definition 📏

Mean Depth:	5.5 m (18 ft)
Max Depth:	9.1 m (30 ft)
Way Point:	44° 30' 00" Lat - N
	77° 53' 00" Lon - W

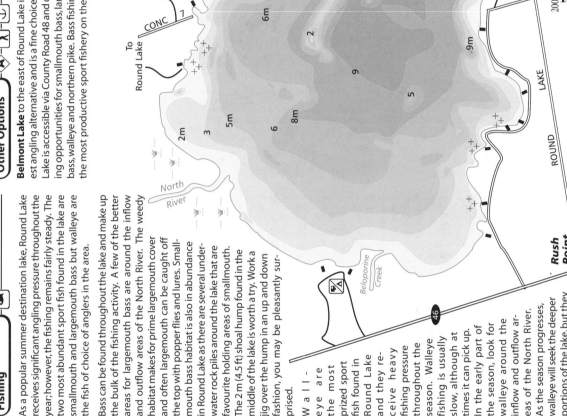

Round Lake Dam

2m
6
Whitney Cr
Sebright Bay
2m
6m
2
.9m
9
5
8m
6
5m
2m
3
CONC 7
To Round Lake
North River
ROAD
ROUND LAKE ROAD
Beloporine Creek
46
Rush Point
To Havelock
To County Rd 48

N

Scale
200m 0 200m 400m 600m 800m 1000m

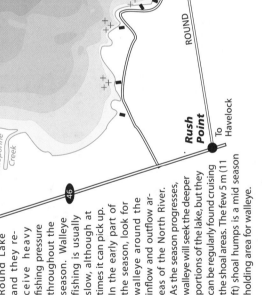

Kawarthas Key

Orillia
Bobcaygeon
Round Lake
Hiawatha
Peterborough
Belleville
Trenton
Tyendinaga
Kingston

Cordova Mines
To Marmora
Blairton Station
Lost Lake
Belmont Lake
PRESTON Rd
7
48
Round Lake
Round Lake
CONC
Rush Point
46
44
To Peterborough

Map Courtesy of Backroad Mapbooks

Salmon Lake

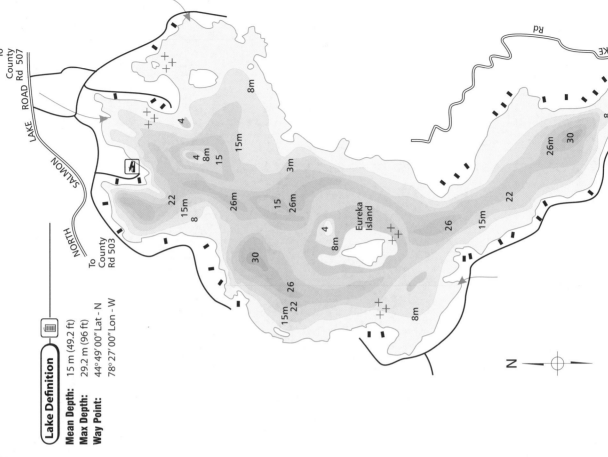

NORTH SALMON LAKE ROAD

To
County
Rd 503

8m

4

4
8m
15

15m

22

15m

8

22

15m
8

30

15

26m

26m

30

4

8m

Eureka
Island

26

22

15m

26

8m

15m
22

SOUTH SALMON LAKE

Rd

26m

30

8

N

Scale

100m   0   100m 200m 300m 400m 500m

Lake Definition

Mean Depth:	15 m (49.2 ft)
Max Depth:	29.2 m (96 ft)
Way Point:	44° 49' 00" Lat - N
	78° 27' 00" Lon - W

Access

Salmon Lake is another fine lake found in the Kawartha Highlands. From the southwest, follow Highway 35 north to the town of Norland. County Road 45 travels east from Norland to the town of Kinmount. At Kinmount, County Road 45 changes to Highway 503. Travel east along Highway 503 to White Lake Road. Take White Lake Road east to the settlement of Fortescue and the junction with the North Salmon Lake Road. Following the North Salmon Lake Road will lead you to Salmon Lake.

North Salmon Lake Road can also be found off Highway 507 to the east.

Fishing

Smallmouth bass provide the majority of the fishing action on Salmon Lake. Smallmouth can be found throughout the lake near rocky drop-offs along the shore and near the two islands. It is also recommended to also look for smallies around any one of the underwater rock piles found around the lake. An area that is known to hold some lunker smallmouth is the 4 m (9 ft) shoal hump found just north of Eureka Island.

The other main sport fish species is lake trout. Lake trout were stocked in Salmon Lake up until the early 1990's to supplement natural populations. Today, Salmon Lake relies on natural reproduction for its lakers, enhancing the need for catch and release. Be sure to check the regulations before fishing on Salmon Lake, as there are slot size and ice fishing restrictions in place to aid the fragile lake trout stocks.

Facilities

There is a public boat launch located along the northern shore of Salmon Lake that can be reached via an access road off the North Salmon Lake Road. For supplies, the town of Kinmount has plenty to offer.

Other Options

If you take White Lake Road en route to Salmon Lake, you will pass the southern end of Salerno Lake approximately 2 km west of North Salmon Lake Road. **Salerno Lake** is another cottage destination lake in the area that offers decent fishing for visitors. The lake is inhabited by mainly smallmouth bass but there are reports of largemouth bass lurking in the shallower areas. Walleye and muskellunge round out the angling options in Salerno Lake.

Kawarthas Key

Salmon
Lake
Orillia   Bobcaygeon
Peterborough
Hiawatha   Belleville
Trenton   Tyendinaga
Kingston

Salerno
Lake
White
Salmon
Lake
Ewan
503
Furnace
Falls
45
Mount
Irwin
Crystal
Lake
1
121
To
Bobcaygeon
Map Courtesy of Backroad Mapbooks

Sandy Lake (Harvey Twp)

Access

Sandy Lake is a part of the large chain of Kawartha Lakes that stretches from the Trenton area to Orillia. Since it is not part of the Trent Severn Waterway, Sandy Lake is not as busy as some of the lakes in the area. The lake lies just to the north of Buckhorn Lake and is accessible via cottage roads west of the town of Buckhorn. To reach Buckhorn, take Highway 28 north of Lindsay to Burleigh Falls. At Burleigh falls, follow County Road 36 west all the way to Buckhorn.

Other Options

Since Sandy Lake lies in the midst of the Trent Severn Kawartha Lakes, there are plenty of accessible angling options close by. **Buckhorn Lake** to the south and the **Bald Lakes** to the north are two fine fishing alternatives. Healthy populations of smallmouth bass, largemouth bass, walleye and muskellunge inhabit both lake systems.

Fishing

As a more out-of-the-way lake, the fishing in Sandy Lake is said to be better than in the lakes of the Trent Severn Waterway. Sandy Lake is home to several cottages and camps, but still maintains its rough nature lustre. Smallmouth and largemouth bass are the two most abundant sport fish found in the lake and fishing can be good at times. Walleye remain main fishing attraction and can be found in fair to good numbers. Muskellunge round out the large sport fish specimens in Sandy Lake and are available in small to fair numbers.

Sandy Lake is a very unique lake due to the fact that it is spring fed, which is a rarity in this region. The spring fed nature of the lake has resulted in water clarity that is unlike any other Kawartha lake and a water colour that is almost turquoise in nature. The lake also has a very diverse bottom structure. One glance at the depth chart will reveal several 2-4 m (6-13 ft) shoals around the lake. These shoals are ideal holding areas for baitfish and as a result, good locations to try your luck for predators such as walleye or muskellunge. Try stationary jigging or trolling over one of these shoals to target walleye and musky.

Facilities

Along with the numerous cottages and camps, there is a tent and trailer park available on the north eastern shore. Boat access is provided at the tent and trailer park or at the southeast end of the lake. For basic supplies, the town of Buckhorn is not far away or alternatively, you can travel back to Lakefield for more services.

Lake Definition

Mean Depth: 6.1m (20.1 ft)
Max Depth: 12.9 m (42.3 ft)
Way Point: 114° 32' 00" Lat - N
78° 25' 00" Long - W

Kawarthas Key

Map Courtesy of Backroad Mapbooks

Shadow Lake

Access

Shadow Lake is found next to the town of Norland, just off Highway 35. To find the lake, simply follow Highway 35 north from Lindsay to Norland. Look for the signs in town directing you from the highway to the access areas on the lake.

Facilities

There is a main boat launch area in the town of Norland along the northwest side of Shadow Lake. Alternatively, there is a more rustic car top access further down from the boat launch. For overnight accommodations, there are two tent and trailer parks located on the lake. For more established camping, **Balsam Lake Provincial Park** can be found within minutes of Norland to the south off County Road 48. The provincial park offers everything from showers to flush toilets, although can be busy in the summer. Call (888) ONT-PARK for reservations.

Fishing

Shadow Lake is a well developed cottage destination lake that experiences some significant fishing pressure throughout the year. Fishing is best for smallmouth and largemouth bass. Bass can be found around shore structure such as cottage docks or rocky shoreline. Look for both species off any one of the islands found around the lake.

Walleye are the most heavily fished sport fish species in Shadow Lake and provide for generally fair fishing much of the time. Walleye average about 0.5-1.5 kg (1-3.5 lbs) on the lake. Some recommended walleye holding areas are off any of the large shoal areas found in the middle of the lake or around the 2 m (4 ft) shoal hump in the north end. In both cases, try to locate some weed structure, as walleye will cruise these areas in search of baitfish. In spring, walleye can be found regularly in the shoal areas but in the summer, they tend to frequent the shoals only during the evening or heavy overcast periods.

Muskellunge are also found in Shadow Lake but fishing success is marginal. Anglers who hook into a musky can expect a fish that averages about 3-4 kg (7-9 lbs) in size.

Other Options

To the north of Shadow Lake, the rolling terrain begins to become more rustic compared to the Norland area. This region is home to countless fishing lakes, including Gull Lake, which is about found 10 km north of Norland just off the highway. **Gull Lake** is a large lake that offers fishing opportunities for largemouth bass, smallmouth bass and lake trout.

Lake Definition

Mean Depth: 11.5 m (37.9 ft)
Max Depth: 22 m (72.1 ft)
Way Point: 44°43'00" Lat - N
78°48'00" Long - W

Kawarthas Key

Silver Lake

Access

North of the town of Coboconk, Silver Lake can be accessed just off the east side of Highway 35. Although the lake itself can be seen from the highway, the main access is found to the north on Shadow Lake at the town of Norland. In Norland, there are signs on Highway 35 that can easily direct you to the boat launch onto Shadow Lake. From the access area, you must travel south via Shadow Lake then along the meandering Gull River to access Silver Lake.

Facilities

Although Silver Lake is a highly developed lake, there are no immediate amenities found on the lake. Supplies can be picked up in either the town of Norland or Coboconk, while there are a few motels in the area that offer overnight accommodation.

Fishing

The main sport fish that inhabit this warm water lake are bass, walleye and muskellunge. Fishing for bass is best, as smallmouth bass and largemouth bass are both found in the lake in good numbers. Both bass species are mainly located along the shoreline area. Smallmouth can be found deeper than largemouth off rock drop-offs around the lake. The inflow of the Gull River is often a high producing area.

Although they are the preferred species, fishing for walleye and muskellunge is much slower than for bass. Walleye average about 0.5-1.5 kg (1-3.5 lbs) in size and can be found near the Gull River inflow and outflow areas mainly in spring. As the summer sets in, look for walleye off the large shoal area in the eastern portion of the lake. Locating underwater vegetation is essential in producing consistent results for walleye on this lake. Ardent musky anglers will tell you the lake is a pleasure to fish but the average angler may not find too many musky in Silver Lake.

Other Options

Via Highway 35, you can reach a multitude of fishing lakes found north of Silver and Shadow Lakes. Only minutes away, you will pass by **Moore Lake** and **Gull Lake**, both accessible from the highway. Both lakes offer fishing for smallmouth bass, largemouth bass and lake trout. As with most Kawartha area lakes, lake trout populations are quite low.

Lake Definition

Mean Depth: 11.5 m (37.9 ft)
Max Depth: 22 m (72.1 ft)
Way Point: 44° 41' 00" Lat - N
78° 48' 00" Long - W

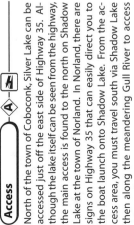

Kawarthas Key

Map Courtesy of Backroad Mapbooks

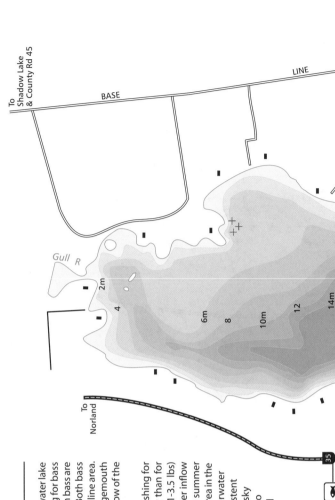

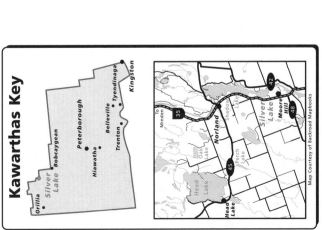

To Shadow Lake & County Rd 45

BASE LINE ROAD

To Hwy 35

N

Gull River

Gull R

2m
4
6m
8
10m
12
14m
16

To Norland

KELVIN-ROCK Dr

35

To Coboconk & Balsam Lake

100m   0   100m 200m 300m 400m 500m
Scale

Spring Lake

Access

You can find this small lake off the east side of Highway 62 south of the town of Bancroft. A rough public access is found off the highway.

Other Options

A very close by alternative fishing lake is Robinson Lake to the southwest. **Robinson Lake** is also accessible off Highway 62 and provides steady fishing for smallmouth bass and the odd stocked lake trout.

Fishing

Even though Spring Lake lies along Highway 62, the lake is not heavily fished. The lake has been stocked with rainbow trout in the past; although success for these trout was somewhat limited. Recently, the stocking program has been changed to splake, although the results are still sketchy. Try ice fishing during the winter or trolling small silver spoons during the spring. During summer, the splake revert to the depths of the lake and can be found around the two deep holes.

Smallmouth bass are also found in Spring Lake and are best located along weed lines or off the main island. All the typical bass lures will work for these smallmouth, although they can be finicky at times. When the success is slow, try working a jig or similar type bait off the bottom near underwater weed or rock structure. A slower presentation will often entice strikes from lethargic bass.

Facilities

Along with the public access along the western shore of the lake, the Hastings Heritage Trail passes along the eastern shore. The trail is a terrific multi-purpose recreation route that is quite popular in the winter with snowmobilers. The trail was originally a rail line and currently stretches from near Algonquin Park south all the way to the town of Trenton.

Lake Definition

Mean Depth: 4.8 m (16 ft)
Max Depth: 9 m (30 ft)
Way Point: 44° 53' 00" Lat - N
77° 43' 00" Lon - W

Stocking Info

Fish Species	Number
Rainbow Trout	3,000
Splake	1,000

Kawarthas Key

Map Courtesy of Backroad Mapbooks

St Ola Lake

Access

St Ola Lake is actually an extension of the larger Limerick Lake to the north. The lakes are found near Highway 62 north of Madoc. Continue on Highway 62 north past the settlement of Gilmour to St. Ola Road. St. Ola Road traverses east from Highway 62 all the way to the southern shore of the lake.

Fishing

St Ola Lake is a part of a collection of fine bass lakes found in the area. The lake is formed by the damming of the Mephisto Creek and is quite shallow, making for prime bass habitat. Along with largemouth bass, smallmouth bass are also found in the lake, although in smaller numbers. There is literally an endless array of weed structure available to fish, making for prime top water situations. Popper flies or top water lures such as the jitterbug can produce some fun action on St Ola Lake. Top water action is mainly found during overcast or dusk periods; therefore, a deeper presentation such as a jig is best when the bass are holding deep. Jig type baits are perfect for this type of lake as they are much harder to snag and can be worked through the thick vegetation where the bigger fish hang out.

Other Options

If you continue east along St Ola Road past St Ola Lake you eventually reach Weslemkoon Lake Road. Take Weslemkoon Lake Road north about 2 km to **Gunter Lake.** Gunter Lake offers fishing for some nice sized largemouth bass.

Facilities

From the St. Ola Road, you can reach the boat launch area as well as a tent and trailer park. Both of these facilities are accessible via short access roads that branch north off St. Ola Road. For supplies, there is a very small store just off the highway at Gilmour.

Lake Definition

Mean Depth: 3 m (9.8 ft)
Max Depth: 3.6 m (12 ft)
Way Point: 44° 52' 00" Lat - N
77° 37' 00" Long - W

To St Ola Rd

St Ola Dam

Mephisto Creek

OLA Rd

St Ola Rd

St. Ola

To Hwy 62

Limerick Lake

N

100m 0 100m 200m 300m 400m 500m

— Scale —

Kawarthas Key

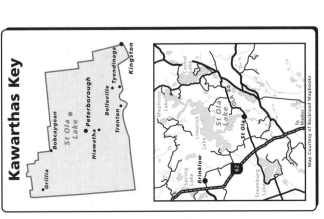

Map Courtesy of Backroad Mapbooks

Stoco Lake

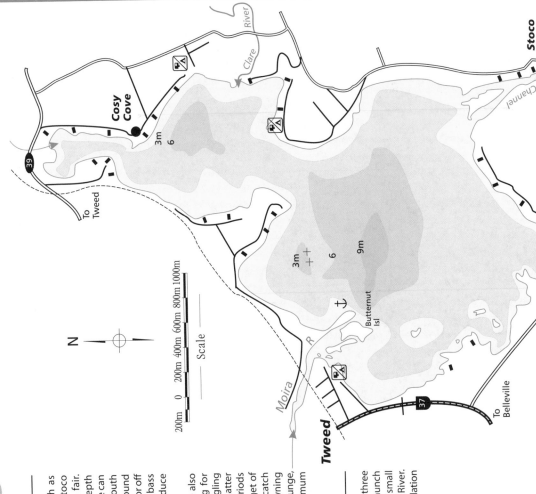

Access

This fabulous lake makes up the scenic eastern boundary of the town of Tweed. The lake is easily accessible, as there are several directional signs that can be spotted in town that lead to parts of the lake. Tweed can be reached via Highway 37. Highway 37 can be picked up to the south from Highway 401 near Belleville or from Highway 7 to the north.

Other Options

The **Moira River** is an angling alternative that cannot be overlooked. The large river flows into and out of Stoco Lake and both the northern and southern stretches of the river have plenty to offer the angler. The river is easily accessible from numerous areas throughout its entirety. The main sport fish species found in the Moira River are smallmouth bass, largemouth bass, northern pike and the odd muskellunge or walleye.

Fishing

Being close to a summer tourist town such as Tweed increases the angling pressure on Stoco Lake. Currently, the fishing quality remains fair. Stoco Lake is a shallow lake with an average depth of approximately 3 m (10 ft). Fishing in the lake can be good at times for smallmouth and largemouth bass in the 0.5-1.5 kg (1-3.5 lb) range. Bass are found mainly closer to shore structure in weed beds or off any of the small islands on the lake. Typical bass lures such as jigs and spinner baits can produce decent results.

The three predatory fish found in Stoco Lake also receive the most angling attention. Fishing for walleye and northern pike can be fair, while angling success for muskellunge is hit and miss. No matter which species, there are often some slow periods on this lake. Since walleye are the prime target of anglers, be sure to aid the stocks and practice catch and release, especially if you hook into a spawning sized walleye. If you do plan to fish for muskellunge, ensure you check the regulations as new minimum size limits have been recently introduced.

Facilities

The lake is a great summer vacation spot with three tent and trailer parks to choose from. A boat launch is also located along the western shore at a small marina found near the inflow of the Moira River. Any needed supplies and roofed accommodation can be found in the town of Tweed.

Lake Definition

Mean Depth: 6 m (19.6 ft)
Max Depth: 9 m (30 ft)
Way Point: 44°28'00" Lat - N
77°17'00" Long - W

Kawarthas Key

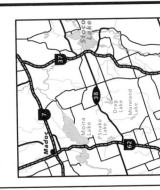

Map Courtesy of Backroad Mapbooks

Stoney (Stony) & Clear Lakes

Access

These lakes are somewhat of a divider between the Great Lake lowlands to the south and the highland areas to the north. The lakes are easily reached by following Highway 28 north from Lakefield. The main access area is from the settlement of Burleigh Falls, home to the 28th Trent Severn Waterway lift lock.

To access the southern portion of the lake or Clear Lake, follow Highway 28 north of the town of Lakefield. Highway 28 passes right by Young's Point, which is the southernmost limit of Clear Lake.

Fishing

Stoney and Clear Lakes lie within the southern extension of the Haliburton/Madawaska Highlands and are characterized by rocky shorelines. There are literally hundreds of small islands around the lake, creating navigational headaches for some boaters. Fishing in the lake is best for smallmouth and largemouth bass. Bass can be found to some good sizes in these Kawartha Lakes and readily cruise around rock structure such as islands or in weedy bays. All the typical assortment of bass lures can provide success, while top water action can be productive at various times. Near the divide between the two lakes, Davis Island is known to produce some nice sized bass.

Walleye and muskellunge are the dominant predators found in the lakes and fishing can be good at times. Both species can be found to decent sizes. With the multitude of islands, weed beds, shoals and quaint bays found around the lakes, the key to success is to find structure. The 4 m (13 ft) shoal areas located south of Big Island on Clear Lake are definitely worth a visit for both of these popular sport fish.

Lake Definition

Mean Depth: 4.7 m (15.5 ft)
Max Depth: 10.6 m (35 ft)
Way Point: 44°28'00"Lat - N
78°43'00"Long - W

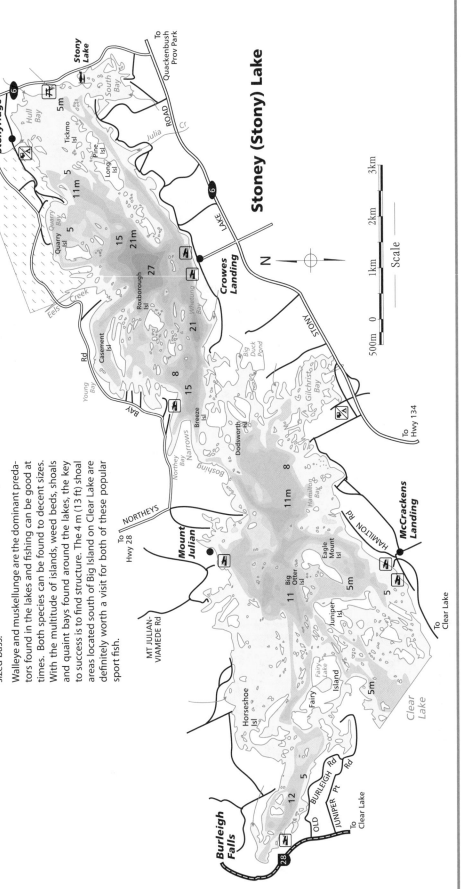

Stoney (Stony) Lake

Stoney (Stony) and Clear Lakes

Facilities

Other Options

Along with the main boat access area in Burleigh Falls, there are several other boat launch areas around the lakes. Crowes Landing and McCrackens Landing are other popular access points to Stoney Lake. Accommodations can be found in Burleigh Falls or at any of the number of tent and trailer parks in the immediate area.

An interesting attraction found near the northeast shore of Stoney Lake is **Petroglyphs Provincial Park**. The park is a day-use park that helps protect ancient native petroglyphs, carvings in rock bed. There is also a picnic area at the park and a few hiking trails. Call (705) 877-2522 for more information.

For a little change, you can access several fishing lakes north of Stoney Lake via Highway 28. There are quality lakes, such as Julian Lake, that can be accessed not far from the highway. Alternatively, if you do not mind a little work, there are literally hundreds of backcountry lakes found to the north that can be reached by 4wd vehicle, canoe or on foot.

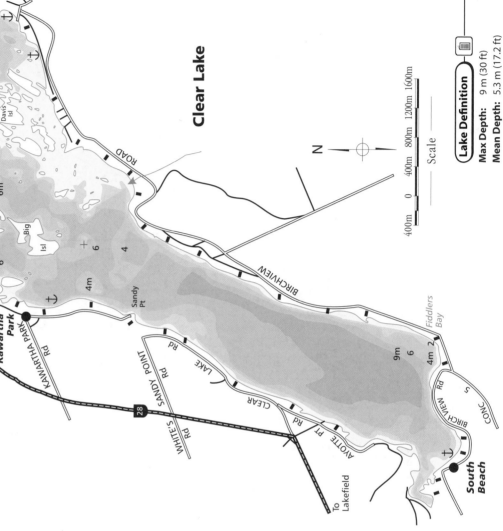

Clear Lake

N

Scale

400m 0 400m 800m 1200m 1600m

Lake Definition

Max Depth: 9 m (30 ft)
Mean Depth: 5.3 m (17.2 ft)
Way Point: 44° 30' 00" Lat - N
78° 12' 00" Lon - W

Kawarthas Key

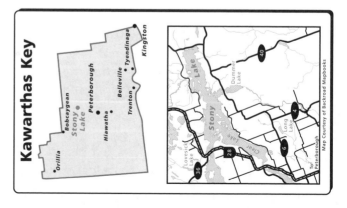

Map Courtesy of Backroad Mapbooks

Sturgeon Lake

Access (west)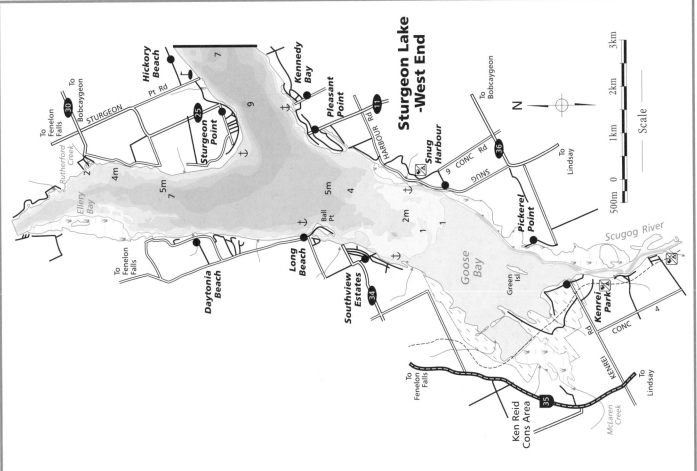

To reach the West End of Sturgeon Lake, there are two main options. One option is to continue north along Highway 35 from the town of Lindsay. The highway actually passes within a few kilometres of the western shore of Sturgeon Lake providing access to the many side roads to the lake.

The other option is to follow County Road 36 from Lindsay. County Road 36 travels north towards the eastern shoreline of Sturgeon Lake. Numerous side roads branch off the county road and provide access to the lake.

Fishing

Walleye are the most sought after sport fish in Sturgeon Lake and fishing for the species is good at times. Walleye are most readily found along shoal areas with some weed growth. Look for weed lines and troll a Rapala or worm harness along these areas to find cruising walleye. Productive areas in the east end of Sturgeon Lake are the shoals around Muskrat Island and Hawkers Bay. In the West End, a renowned hot spot is the region south of Fenelon Falls, including Eldery Bay.

Smallmouth and largemouth bass can be found throughout Sturgeon Lake and are predominantly located along shore structure and near weed beds. In particular, Goose Bay is a prime holding area for bass, especially largemouth bass, due to the heavy weed growth in the bay. In heavier weed cover, try working a jig through the weeds in an up and down jigging motion. Even lethargic bass often suck in the passing jig.

The other main sport fish found in Sturgeon Lake is muskellunge. Fishing for muskellunge is usually fair for nice sized musky. Muskellunge can also be found along weed lines in search of bait fish, especially during the evenings. Larger presentations are needed to lure that big musky. On the flip side, larger lures will limit your incidental catches of other sport fish.

Facilities (west)

Boat access areas are readily available along the west end of Sturgeon Lake. There are several marinas available along the eastern and western shorelines of this stretch of the lake. For camping accommodations, there are tent and trailer parks located at Snug Harbour and south of the **Ken Reid Conservation Area** along the Sturgeon River. The Ken Reid Conservation Area is accessible off Highway 35 north of Lindsay and offers picnic areas, a beach and washrooms for day-trippers. Organized groups can arrange to camp at the conservation area by calling (705) 328-2271.

Kawarthas Key

Map Courtesy of Backroad Mapbooks

Sturgeon Lake

Lake Definition

Mean Depth:	4.7 m (15.5 ft)
Max Depth:	10.6 m (35 ft)
Way Point:	44° 28' 00" Lat - N
	78° 43' 00" Long - W

Access (east)

Sturgeon Lake is part of the Trent Severn Waterway. Many anglers cruise from lake to lake enjoying the many facilities and good fishing along the waterway. Due to the waterway and easy access, Sturgeon Lake can be busy with boating traffic, especially in the summer.

The main access area to the eastern stretch of Sturgeon Lake is via the town of Bobcaygeon. One of the most direct routes to Bobcaygeon is by taking County Road 17 from the town of Lindsay. County Road 17 travels east and eventually veers north to Bobcaygeon. In the town, there is a boat launch and a marina providing access to the lake. To reach Lindsay, take Highway 35 north from Highway 401 east of the town of Bowmanville.

Facilities (east)

There are a number of boat launch facilities that can be found along the eastern portion of Sturgeon Lake. The main launch area is located in the town of Bobcaygeon. Other launch areas are available at Ancona Point and Verulam Park further to the south. For added boating services, there are a few marinas available along this side of the lake. Overnight camping can be found at the tent and trailer park near Bobcaygeon, while roofed accommodation can be found in and around town.

Other Options

Some nearby fishing options include **Pigeon Lake** to the east and **Cameron Lake** to the west. Both lakes are part of the Trent Severn Waterway and are accessible by boat from Sturgeon Lake. Since all the lakes are somewhat interconnected, fishing is comparable to Sturgeon Lake. Populations of smallmouth bass, largemouth bass, walleye and muskellunge inhabit the lakes.

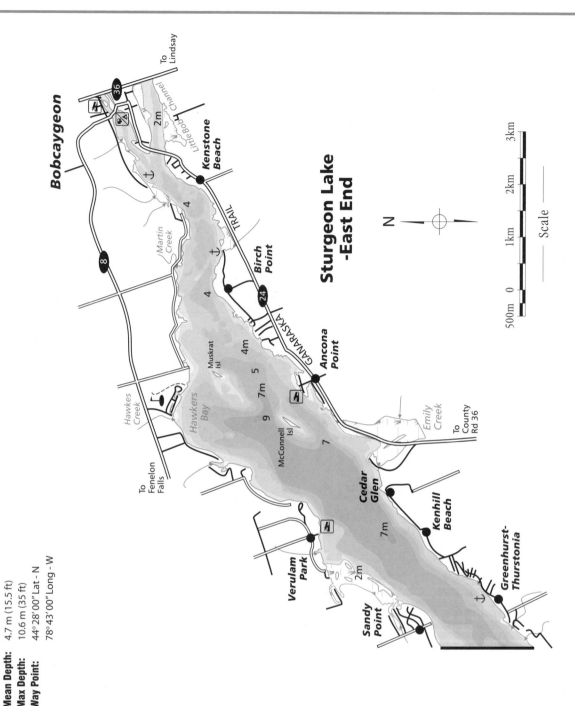

Sturgeon Lake - East End

Bobcaygeon
To Lindsay
36
Little Bob Channel
2m
Kenstone Beach
Martin Creek
4
8
Birch Point
4
24
GANARASKA TRAIL
Muskrat Isl
4m
5
7m
Hawkers Bay
9
Ancona Point
McConnell Isl
7
Emily Creek
To County Rd 36
Hawkes Creek
To Fenelon Falls
Cedar Glen
7m
Verulam Park
Kenhill Beach
2m
Sandy Point
Greenhurst-Thurstonia

N

Scale
500m 0   1km   2km   3km

Sweets Lake

Access

Sweets Lake can be accessed via a rough 2wd road that branches off Highway 62 north of Gilmour. When travelling north along Highway 62, the access road can be noticed by watching for the sign to Steenburg Lake Road North. A few kilometres later, the unmarked access road to Sweets Lake juts off the west side of the highway.

Facilities

There are no amenities at Sweets Lake, although tent and trailer parks can be found to the west on Wollaston Lake or to the east on St Ola Lake. For supplies, the small town of Coe Hill offers a grocery store and a general store. Coe Hill lies to the west of Sweets Lake via County Road 620.

Fishing

This small out of the way lake is home to a few cottages and camps. The lake provides good fishing at times for largemouth bass. Bass can be found throughout the lake near weed structure, which is more prevalent near the lakeshore area. The small creek inlets often dry significantly as the heat of summer approaches and the areas around the mouth of these creeks are usually good producers of water vegetation suitable for bass. During overcast and dusk periods, the bass in Sweets Lake can be caught on the fly with top water poppers or with other surface lures such as the floating Rapala minnow. During slower periods, try working a jig slowly off bottom structure. An up and down motion along the bottom can often entice strikes from otherwise spooky bass.

Other Options

South of Sweets Lake, **Steenburg Lake** can be reached via Steenburg Lake Road North off of Highway 62. There is a boat launch available along the northeast shore of the lake, while both largemouth and smallmouth bass provide the action.

Lake Definition

Perimeter:	2.6 km (1.6 mi)
Mean Depth:	5.1 m (16.9 ft)
Max Depth:	10.7 m (35.1 ft)
Way Point:	44°52'00"Lat - N
	77°44'00"Long - W

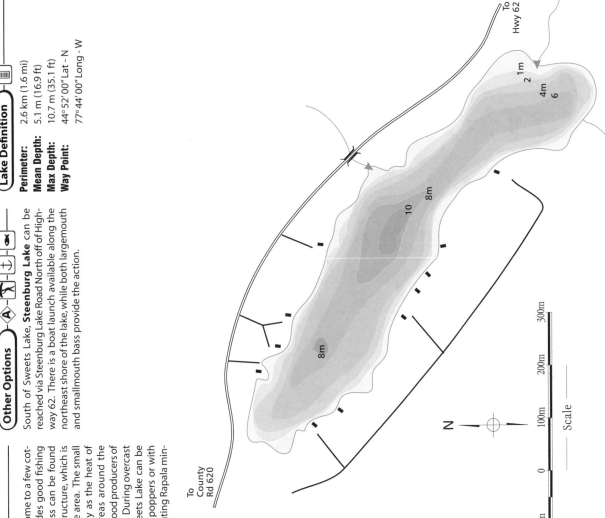

Tallan Lake

Access

North of the town of Apsley, Tallan Lake can be reached by taking County Road 620 east from Highway 28. Look for Clydesdale Road off the north side of County Road 620 and follow Clydesdale Road all the way to Tallan Lake.

Facilities

A boat launch is available along the northern shore of Tallan Lake via an access road from Clydesdale Road. For overnight camping, **Silent Lake Provincial Park** is located north of Tallan Lake via Highway 28. The park is a full service Provincial Park that offers some scenic lakeside campsites along with services such as flush toilets and showers. The park can be busy during the summer months; therefore, it is recommended to make reservations before arrival. For reservations call (888) ONT-PARK.

Fishing

Some cottages and camps line the shoreline of Tallan Lake, hence fishing pressure is steady throughout the year. The resident smallmouth bass make up the brunt of the angling success. Smallmouth bass average approximately 0.5-1 kg (1-2 lbs) and are found mainly near underwater structure such as rock piles or weed areas. Off the island in the west side of the lake is another productive area.

The other main sport fish species found in Tallan Lake is lake trout. The lake trout are a naturally reproducing strain that is under heavy fishing pressure. Regulations on the lake have been imposed, such as slot sizes and winter sanctuary periods to help the struggling lake trout stocks. If you do intend to fish for lakers, please practice catch-and-release.

Other Options

Clydesdale Lake is accessible via Hobson Road from Clydesdale Road southeast of Tallan Lake. Clydesdale Lake is another cottage destination lake in the area that offers fishing opportunities for smallmouth bass.

Lake Definition

Mean Depth: 12.6 m (41.3 ft)
Max Depth: 25.6 m (84 ft)
Way Point: 44°51'00" Lat - N
78°03'00" Long - W

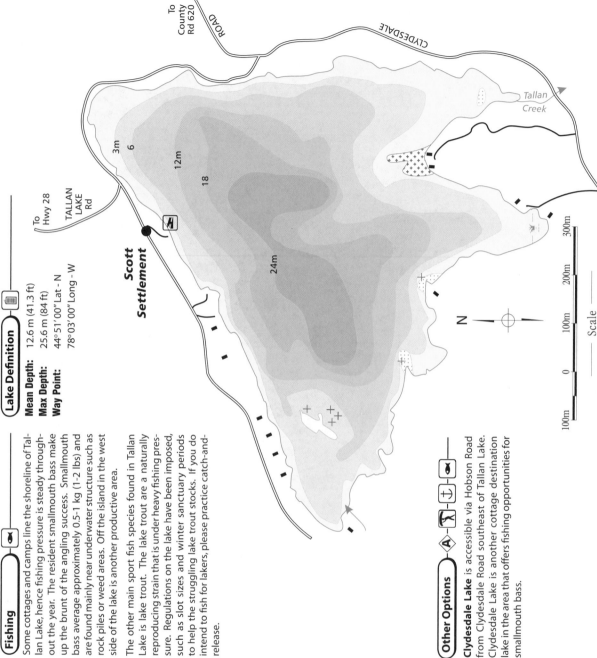

To County Rd 620

CLYDESDALE ROAD

Tallan Creek

To County Rd 620

3m
6
12m
18
24m

To Hwy 28

TALLAN LAKE Rd

Scott Settlement

N

Scale
100m 0 100m 200m 300m

Kawarthas Key

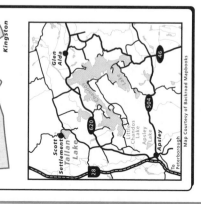

Orillia
Bobcaygeon
Peterborough
Hiawatha
Tallan Lake
Belleville
Trenton
Tyendinaga
Kingston

Glen Alda
Little Chandos Lake
Apsley Lake
Scott Settlement
Tallan Lake
Apsley
To Peterborough

Map Courtesy of Backroad Mapbooks

Tangamong & Whetstone Lakes

Access

This collection of lakes is part of the Crowe River system found between Highway 28 and Highway 62. In addition to the public access point on Tangamong Lake, many paddlers reach the lakes by paddling along the Crowe River.

You can reach the access point on the southern shore of Tangamong Lake via Tangamong Road. To find Tangamong Road, first travel north along Highway 28 to Highway 504 near Apsley. Follow Highway 504 east to County Road 46 and head south. About 4 km south along County Road 46 you will meet Sandy Lake Road, which travels south to the junction with Tangamong Road.

Fishing

Both Tangamong Lake and Whetstone Lake are surrounded by private land. The southern shore of Tangamong Lake is highly developed with cottages and camps. Fishing in the lakes is often productive for smallmouth and largemouth bass that can reach over 1.5 kg (3.5 lbs) in size on occasion. Bass can be found throughout the lakes in weedy areas and off the areas with a rocky shoreline. The narrows between Tangamong Lake and Whetstone Lake is a consistent producer of feisty bass.

The other sport fish found in the lakes is walleye and muskellunge. Success for both predators varies but you can usually expect to catch a few walleye during an outing. The 3 m (10 ft) shoal area located in the northern portion of Tangamong Lake is a known holding area for species. The shallow region offers just the right mix of under water structure to attract feeding walleye and musky. The inflow area around the Crowe River is also a good holding area for walleye and muskellunge, especially in spring. In Whetstone Lake, look for walleye along the weed area near the mouth of the Crowe River. Watch for special restrictions on both lakes.

Other Options

The access and parking area on Tangamong Lake is found on the southern shore of the lake at Tangamong Lodge. There is a small fee for parking and using the canoe/boat launch. Basic supplies and various accommodations are available in and around the town of Apsley. For camping enthusiasts, **Silent Lake Provincial Park** is found to the north of Apsley off Highway 28.

Facilities

At the junction between Sandy Lake Road and Tangamong Road you can easily reach Sandy Lake. The small lake is home to a population of smallmouth bass and muskellunge. Alternatively, further south of **Sandy Lake**, **West Twin Lake** is accessible via County Road 46. West Twin Lake is also inhabited with smallmouth bass and muskellunge as well as largemouth bass.

Lake Definition

Mean Depth: 10.7 m (35.2 ft)
Max Depth: 21 m (70 ft)
Way Point: 44°53'00" Lat - N
75°50'00" Long - W

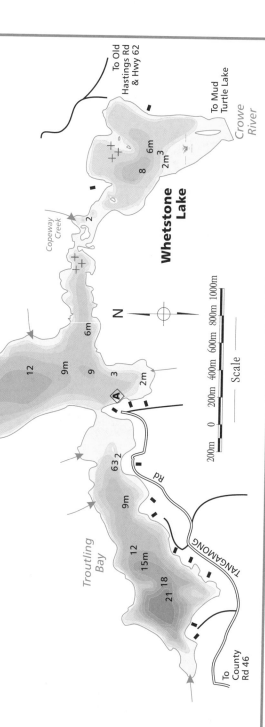

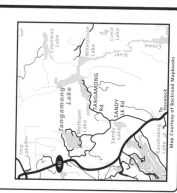

Kawarthas Key

Map Courtesy of Backroad Mapbooks

Thanet Lake

Access

Thanet Lake is sandwiched between Highway 28 to the west and Highway 62 to the east. To reach the lake from the west, travel north along Highway 28 to Highway 504 at the town of Apsley. Follow Highway 504 east through the town of Apsley to the junction with County Road 46. Continue east across County Road 46 along Lasswade Road. Just after you pass Henderson Lake off the north side of Lasswade Road, take the first access road off the south side of the road. If you end up at Murphy Corners, you have gone too far.

From the east, follow Highway 62 north past the pic-nic area on Jordan Lake. The next main road heading west is Steenburg Lake Road North. Follow this road past Murphy Corners and the Dickey Lake turnoff. The next lake to the south is Thanet Lake.

Fishing

There are a few cottages and camps along the shoreline of Thanet Lake, although the lake remains mainly undeveloped. Fishing in the lake is good at times for smallmouth and largemouth bass in the 1 kg (2 lb) range. Around the island found in the east side of the lake is often a good holding area for both smallmouth and largemouth bass. Try casting a jig or spinner towards the island to find ambush ready bass. Top water action can be experienced in any of the quiet bays. Try top water pop-ping flies and lures during dusk or overcast periods for some exciting bass action.

A natural population of lake trout also exist in Thanet Lake, although the population is quite low similar to most Southern Ontario lake trout lakes. Low populations are the direct result of overharvest-ing; hence new regulations on ice fishing and catch sizes have been implemented. Please practice catch-and-release.

Other Options

West Lake can be reached via a short rough portage from the southern end of Thanet Lake. West Lake is surrounded by mainly Crown Land and provides fishing for largemouth bass. Crown Land camping opportunities also exist at the lake.

Facilities

There are no developed facilities available at Thanet Lake but rustic Crown Land camping is certainly possible. For supplies, the town of Apsley has plenty to offer, including a grocery and a general store.

Lake Definition

Elevation: 239 m (785 ft)
Surface Area: 150 ha (371 ac)
Mean Depth: 8.2 m (27.2 ft)
Max Depth: 20.4 m (67 ft)
Perimeter: 10.1 km (6.3 mi)
Way Point: 45°08'00" Lat - N
79°46'00" Lon - W

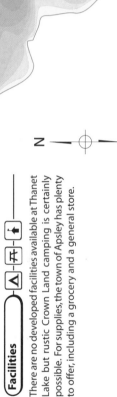

To Henderson Lake

9m
3
18m
21
24m
15m
18
9m
12
6
3m

N

Scale

100m 0 100m 200m 300m 400m 500m

Kawarthas Key

Orillia
Bobcaygeon
Thanet Lake
Peterborough
Hiawatha
Belleville
Trenton
Tyendinaga
Kingston

To Bancroft
62
Ormsby
Steenburg Lake
Steenburg
Dickey Lake
Brett Lake
Glanmire
Wollaston Lake
Urbach Lake
Thanet Lake
Freen Lake
Copeway Lake
Coe Hill
620
Gilroy Lake

Map Courtesy of Backroad Mapbooks

Turtle Lake

Access

Turtle Lake is part of a remote access chain of lakes that can only be found by canoe and portage. The canoe put in is located at the end of Long Lake Road off Highway 28 just south of Apsley. Parking is available for a nominal fee at Long Lake Lodge. To find Turtle Lake, you must paddle west along Long Lake and pass through Loucks Lake then Cox Lake. In total, the trip involves about three portages, with the largest being the 1,503 m (4,931 ft) hike from Cox Lake to Turtle Lake.

Facilities

As an interior access lake, rustic Crown Land campsites dot the landscape. The sites are quite basic, with only a rough fire pit and perhaps a pit toilet. They offer a fantastic way to get away from it all and to enjoy the great outdoors.

Fishing

Since Turtle Lake is an interior access lake, the lake receives significantly less angling pressure than other more accessible lakes in the region. Fishing in the lake can be quite good at times for smallmouth bass in the 0.5-1 kg (1-2 lb) range. Lunker bass are landed annually.

Turtle Lake is a deep lake carved out of the surrounding hills. There are a number of rocky shoreline drop-offs that make perfect habitat for smallmouth bass. Another recommended area to sample is near the small rock island found in the middle of the lake. Try working a jig or similar type lure closer to the bottom for those big smallies. For fly anglers, one fly that is sure to produce results on Turtle Lake is the crayfish imitation. Work the fly off bottom structure in a long quick strip fashion. At times this method can be deadly for smallmouth.

Other Options

There are several lakes in and about the area to sample. **Cox Lake** is another interior access lake found to the north. It offers both largemouth and smallmouth bass as well as stocked lake trout. Fishing is reported to be good.

Lake Definition

Mean Depth:	6.5 m (21.3 ft)
Max Depth:	11.3 m (37 ft)
Way Point:	44°39'00"Lat - N
	78°15'00"Lon - W

To Stoplog Lake

To Cherry Lake

N

Scale

100m 0 100m 200m 300m

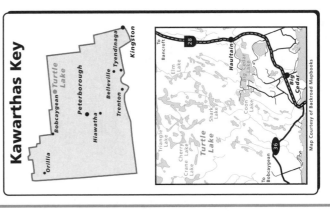

Kawarthas Key

Orillia
Bobcaygeon · Turtle Lake
Peterborough
Hiawatha
Belleville
Trenton · Tyendinaga
Kingston

To Bancroft
Elm Lake
Haultain
Big Cedar
Coon Lake
Shark Lake
Triangle Lake
Cherry Lake
Crane Lake
Turtle Lake
To Bobcaygeon

Map Courtesy of Backroad Mapbooks

Twin Sister Lakes

Access

Twin Sister Lakes are part of a series of lakes that help form the Crowe River system. The road leading north to Thompson Lake separates them. You can find the Twin Sister Lakes by following Highway 7 to the town of Marmora. At the town of Marmora, take County Road 33 north from Highway 7. Follow County Road 33 north to Long Swamp Road. Long Swamp Road is essentially an extension of County Road 33 and traverses north to Twin Sisters Road and Twin Sister Lakes.

Fishing

The Twin Sister Lakes are two side-by-side lakes that are of similar size and fishing quality. There are a few cottages and camps found along the shorelines of both lakes. The main sport fish found are largemouth bass and smallmouth bass. Fishing for both bass species can be good at times for average sized fish. There is plenty of weed structure in the lakes that provide good cover for ambush ready bass. Try flipping a jig through the deeper weed growth, while top water flies and lures can be productive for more aggressive bass. Walleye and muskellunge are also known to exist in the lakes, although fishing for both species is relatively slow.

Facilities

There are no facilities at the Twin Sister Lakes, although any needed supplies can be easily found in the town of Marmora. For overnight accommodation, there are three tent and trailer parks located on the shore of nearby Crowe Lake. For roofed accommodation, there are a few motels that can be found along Highway 7 near the town of Marmora.

Other Options

Just east of Twin Sister Lakes lies **Cordova Lake**. Cordova Lake can be accessed via Vansickle Road from County Road 48. There is a tent and trailer park on the lake and fishing can be decent for both smallmouth bass and walleye. There are rumours of largemouth bass in the lake as well.

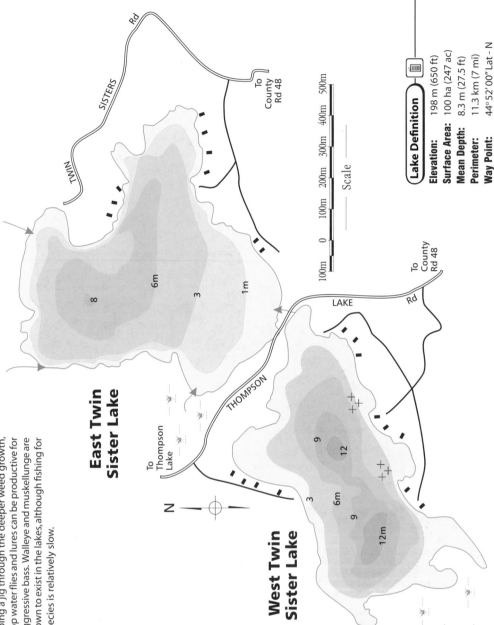

East Twin Sister Lake

West Twin Sister Lake

Lake Definition

Elevation: 198 m (650 ft)
Surface Area: 100 ha (247 ac)
Mean Depth: 8.3 m (27.5 ft)
Perimeter: 11.3 km (7 mi)
Way Point: 44°52'00" Lat - N
79°39'00" Lon - W

Kawarthas Key

Orillia
Bobcaygeon
Twin Sister Lake
Peterborough
Hiawatha
Belleville
Trenton
Tyendinaga
Kingston

Map Courtesy of Backroad Mapbooks

Urbach Lake

Access ⚐ ⚡

Urbach Lake is a remote lake that lies south of the village of Coe Hill. To find the lake, follow Highway 28 north to Highway 620 at the town of Apsley. Take Highway 620 east past Apsley to the village of Coe Hill. As you travel east past Coe Hill, take the first road south after the crossing of the Deer River. This road skirts Wollaston Lake. After about 3 km (2 mi) south along the access road, look for the branch road off the east side that leads to the tiny Urbach Lake.

Facilities ⚐ ⛺ 🚻

There are no facilities available at Urbach Lake. Overnight camping can be found at the tent and trailer park located north of the lake along the northern shore of Wollaston Lake. Basic supplies can be found in Coe Hill.

Fishing 🎣

At first glance, Urbach Lake appears to be a very shallow lake that may only support coarse fish species or at best largemouth bass. On the contrary, Urbach Lake is heavily stocked every few years with splake, the lake trout/speckled trout hybrid species. The stocked splake reportedly provide for some good fishing throughout the ice fishing and during spring fishing periods. The dense population of catchable splake readily strike small spoons jigged through the ice or when trolled in the spring. Summer angling success is much slower, although can be productive by trolling through the deep hole in the lake. Morning or evening, seem to be best if trolling for splake during the summer.

Other Options ⚐ 🎣 ⚓ 🛶 🎣

If you approach Urbach Lake from County Road 629, you will pass **Wollaston Lake**. Wollaston Lake is a cottage destination lake that is home to a boat launch and tent and trailer park. Largemouth bass, smallmouth bass and lake trout are resident in the lake. Watch for special regulations on lake trout as the population levels are very low.

Lake Definition 🗄

Mean Depth:	6 m (19.6 ft)
Max Depth:	12 m (39.4 ft)
Way Point:	44° 50' 00" Lat - N
	77° 49' 00" Lon - W

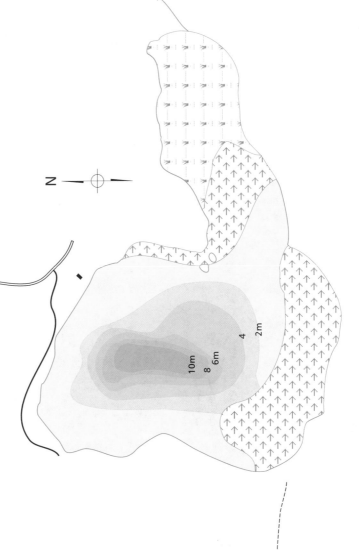

N

To Wollaston Lake & County Rd 620

10m
8
6m
4
2m

100m   0   100m   200m   300m

Scale

Stocking Info

Fish Species	Number
Splake	435

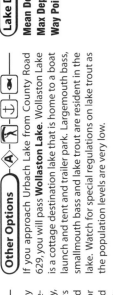

Kawarthas Key

Orillia
Bobcaygeon
Urbach Lake
Peterborough
Hiawatha
Belleville
Trenton
Tyendinaga
Kingston

To Bancroft
62
Steenburg Lake
Ormsby
Brett Lake
Urbach Steenburg Lake
Glanmire
Coe Hill
Dickey Lake
Thanet Lake
Freen Lake
620
Wollaston Lake
Copeway Lake
Gilroy Lake

Map Courtesy of Backroad Mapbooks

Victoria & West Victoria (Wolf) Lakes

Access

Victoria and West Victoria Lakes are hike-in lakes that are found in the wetlands northwest of Norland. The lakes lie next to the popular, long distance Ganaraska Trail. The eastern trailhead can be found by following Highway 35 north from Lindsay past Norland to Moore Falls. At Moore Falls take County Road 2 (Deep Bay Road) north off Highway 35. Follow Deep Bay Road to a rough access road off the west side of Deep Bay Road, just north of Deep Bay. The access road leads to Lutterworth Lake and a parking area for the trail. Victoria Lake lies approximately 9-10 kilometres from this trailhead, while West Victoria Lake is a short jaunt to the west.

Facilities

Both of these lakes are remote fishing lakes that have no formal facilities available. There are a few rustic Crown Land campsites that have been established over the years. If you do intend to camp at the lakes, be sure to practice low impact camping and please remove any garbage that you bring in or may find.

Fishing

With the only real access from the Ganaraska Trail, these lakes receive low angling pressure throughout the season. Fishing is known to be productive for both smallmouth and largemouth bass. Look for bass along shore structure, which is abundant around the lakes. Most of the regular bass lures will produce results, including spinner baits, jigs and top water lures. Fly anglers will find these lakes a treat to fish, as the bass are often easy to entice on top water poppers. A good streamer can also work well when the bass are reluctant to come to the top.

In addition to bass, West Victoria Lake is stocked regularly with splake, which provide for good fishing at times through the ice in winter. A good ice fishing location is off any of the two points along the southern shore of the lake opposite the deep hole. Try jigging a white jig or small silver spoon to entice strikes. Success for splake can also be steady in the spring just after ice off but summer fishing can be very slow.

Other Options

While hiking along the Ganaraska Trail, you will pass other remote lakes including Sheldon Lake. **Sheldon Lake** is a Crown Land lake that offers rustic camping and angling opportunities for smallmouth bass and stocked lake trout. The lake is one of the first larger lakes along the trail and is found approximately 3 km west from the parking area at Lutterworth Lake.

Lake Definition

Mean Depth:	9.4 m (31 ft)
Max Depth:	22.5 m (73.8 ft)
Way Point:	44° 51' 00" Lat - N
	78° 55' 00" Lon - W

Kawarthas Key

Map Courtesy of Backroad Mapbooks

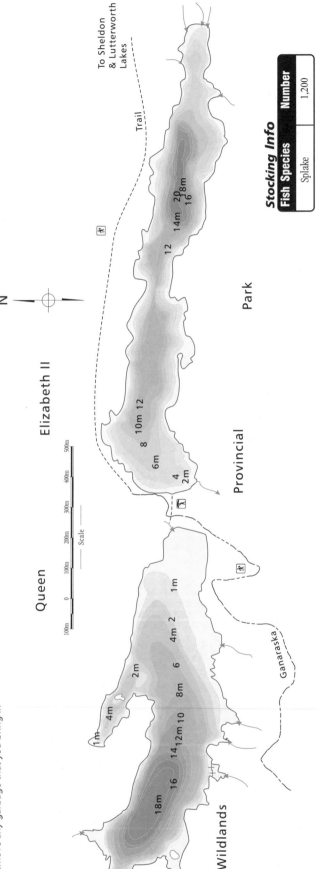

Stocking Info

Fish Species	Number
Splake	1,200

Wellers Bay (Lake Ontario)

Access

Wellers Bay is part of the renowned Lake Ontario and is a popular wildlife viewing area. To reach Wellers Bay you must first travel to the town of Trenton, which is accessible via Highway 401 west of Belleville. From Trenton, follow County Road 33 south to the town of Consecon and the junction with County Road 39. Take County Road 39 west to the main access area along the south side of the bay.

Facilities

You can find a boat launch just west of Consecon as well as north of Consecon off Smoke Point Road. Along with the boat launch areas, there are a few tent and trailer parks available around the lake. A popular tenting area is the region near Bercovan Beach along the north side of the bay. For supplies and lodging, such as bed and breakfasts, the town of Consecon has plenty to offer visitors.

Fishing

Wellers Bay offers fishing opportunities for mainly bass, walleye and northern pike. Both smallmouth and largemouth bass are found in the bay in fair to good numbers and fishing can be quite productive at times. Bass can reach up to 2 kg (4.5 lbs) and there is definitely a possibility of finding a lunker out there. The many weedy areas around the bay make for prime bass habitat. Look for largemouth bass hunkered in weed beds, while smallmouth tend to frequent underwater structure areas such as shoals, logs or rock piles.

Walleye are the most prized sport fish in the bay and success can be steady at times for some nice sized walleye. Look for walleye along weed lines or along shoal areas. Jigging is a proven, effective method in the region. The key is to find the structure where the walleye are more frequently located near.

Northern pike can be picked up almost anywhere in the bay, although they tend to cruise the shallows at dusk or during overcast periods. Some big pike can be found in Weller's Bay and it is possible to hook into pike in the 5 kg (11 lb) range.

If the fishing is slow for the bigger sport fish, you should be able to find some action in the shallower areas for a variety of pan fish including perch and rock bass. The odd rainbow trout and salmon are also caught periodically in the bay.

Other Options

There are a number of different fishing alternatives close by to Wellers Bay, including Consecon Lake, the Bay of Quinte and even Lake Ontario. All three water bodies have plenty to offer anglers. **Consecon Lake** and the **Bay of Quinte** offer fishing opportunities for mainly bass, walleye and northern pike, while in **Lake Ontario** you can also find rainbow trout and salmon. For added success, there are a number of boat charters in the region that offer fully guided outings on the Bay of Quinte and Lake Ontario.

Kawarthas Key

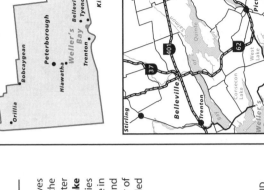

Map Courtesy of Backroad Mapbooks

Lake Definition

Mean Depth:	4.6 m (15 ft)
Max Depth:	7.3 m (24 ft)
Way Point:	44°01'00"Lat - N
	77°36'00"Lon - W

West Lake

Fishing

West Lake is a shallow lake that has plenty of weed growth and other cover throughout the lake. Similar to most Quinte area lakes, West Lake is hit hard for its walleye, although fishing can be fair at times. Look for walleye along weed lines and off the south side of Tubbs Island on occasion. Trolling a worm harness can be effective in a lake like West Lake due to its heavy weed structure. You can literally work the worm harness bait right through weeds. Crankbaits, jigs and other similar baits can also be productive.

Smallmouth and largemouth bass are the two most active sport fish found in West Lake. There is plenty of prime structure to spawn, grow and hide in. Top water action can be exciting at the right times but a tube jig may be the perfect lure to work through the weeds. If your luck is not as productive in the weed beds, try off rock pile structures, such as the rocky shoal found near Tubbs Island.

Some decent sized northern pike are also found in West Lake.

Access

The western shore of West Lake is actually part of the popular Sandbanks Provincial Park, which separates the water body from Lake Ontario. To find the lake follow Highway 401 to Belleville and head south along Highway 62. The smaller highway eventually intersects County Road 33. The county road leads west along the northern shore of the lake. There is a boat access near Wellington as well as on the southeast shore of the lake on Tubbs Island.

Other Options

The nearby cousin to West Lake is **East Lake**, which can be found to the southeast. East Lake can be reached by following County Road 33 to Picton, then by heading south along County Road 10. East Lake has a boat launch and tent and trailer park for visitors to enjoy while the lake offers fishing opportunities for smallmouth bass, largemouth bass, northern pike and walleye.

Facilities

The main attraction to West Lake is **Sandbanks Provincial Park**. The park is one of the most popular provincial parks in the Ontario park system due the massive sand dunes that the park encompasses. The beautiful sandy beaches are a great spot to catch some rays during the heat of summer. For campers, the park offers maintained campsites, flush toilets and showers. The park can be busy; therefore, it is recommended to call (888) ONT-PARK for reservations prior to arrival.

The lake also hosts a boat launch on Tubbs Island as well as a private campground along the eastern shore. Other accommodations and supplies can be found in the village of Wellington.

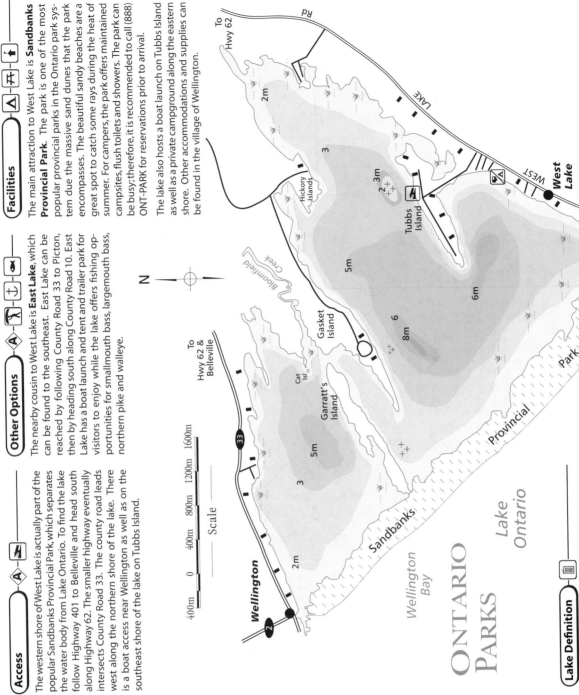

Ontario Parks

Lake Definition

Mean Depth: 4.8 m (15.7 ft)
Max Depth: 7.6 m (25 ft)
Way Point: 43°55'00" Lat - N
77°16'00" Lon - W

Kawarthas Key

Map Courtesy of Backroad Mapbooks

White Lake

Access ⛟ ⚡

White Lake is part of a series of cottage lakes found between Highways 35 and 28, not far from the community of Fortescue. From the west, take Highway 35 north to the town of Norland and turn east onto County Road 45. Follow this country road to the town of Kinmount where the road essentially changes to Highway 503. Continue east along Highway 503 to White Lake Road. Follow White Lake Road east all the way to the rough access near the dam on the north side of the lake. The access is basically suitable for a canoe only. Be sure to watch for private property.

Fishing ⛟

A few cottages can be found along the shore of White Lake, although the fishing pressure is not overly heavy throughout the year. The most active fishing is for smallmouth and largemouth bass, which can be found to some good sizes on occasion. Largemouth can be found in the long weedy bays hunkered beneath the vegetation ready to ambush top water or subsurface presentations. The southwest bay is also a fine holder of nice size largemouth bass. Smallmouth are often picked up off the two large points that jut out into the lake as well as off the large island. Muskellunge is the other main sport fish found in White Lake. Fishing is relatively slow for musky, although picks up in the fall period.

Facilities ⛺ 🎪 🚻

There is a boat launch at the dam site found at the north end of the lake. The nearest tent and trailer park is on the shore of Shadow Lake just south of Norland. Supplies and other necessities can also be picked up in Norland.

Other Options ⛺ 🎣 ⚓ 🐟

Salerno Lake is a popular cottage destination lake that lies due north of White Lake. There are two distinct access roads to **Salerno Lake** that branch north off White Lake Road. The L shaped lake is inhabited by smallmouth bass, walleye, and muskellunge and to a lesser degree largemouth bass. Fishing is best for smallmouth bass, although die-hard musky anglers can often be found frequenting the lake in search of the big predatory game fish.

Lake Definition 📖

Surface Area: 175 ha (432 ac)
Mean Depth: 3.7 m (12.2 ft)
Max. Depth: 10.4 m (34 ft)
Elevation: 305 m (1,002 ft)
Perimeter: 7.6 km (4.7 mi)
Way Point: 44° 50'00"Lat - N 78° 29'00"Lon - W

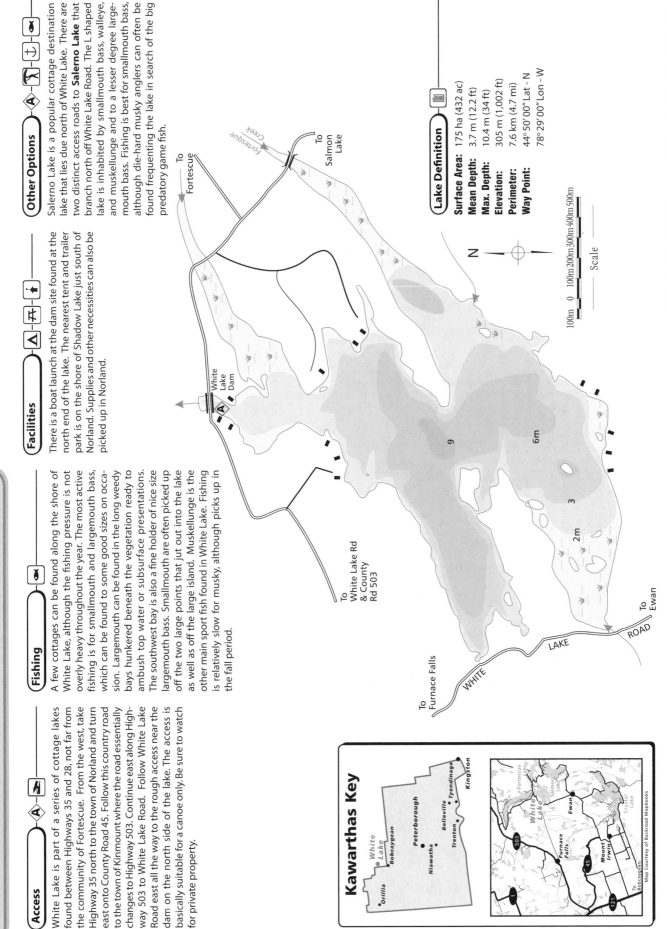

Kawarthas Key

Map Courtesy of Backroad Mapbooks

White Lake

97

Wolf Lake

Access

This smaller Kawartha Lake is located north of Dalrymple Lake near the village of Sebright. To find the lake from the southwest, first follow Highway 12 to the town of Orillia. In the east end of Orillia, you can find County Road 44 off the north side of Highway 12. Take County Road 44 north approximately 4 km to County Road 45 (Monk Road). Follow County Road 45 east across County Road 169 and past the village of Sebright to the eastern shore of Young Lake. The lake is about 2 km north of Sebright.

Fishing

Wolf Lake is riddled with rocky shoreline and underwater areas providing ideal structure for the resident largemouth and smallmouth bass. Coupled with the many small islands around the lake, bass have plenty of area to hide in wait for passing bait. Try working jigs off rocky drop-offs or off the bottom near rock shoals. You may be surprised by the size of some of these bass. Muskellunge are also resident in Wolf Lake but fishing success is usually slow for the large predator.

Other Options

At the town of Sebright, if you follow Boundary Road (County Road 6) north, you will eventually reach **Riley Lake** and **Kashe Lake**. Both lakes are set amid rockier and rolling terrain than the flatter terrain found near Young Lake and Dalrymple Lake to the south. The northern lakes offer fishing opportunities for smallmouth and largemouth bass, while a population of walleye and muskellunge also inhabits Kashe Lake.

Facilities

There is a local community centre along the eastern shore of Young Lake, as well as a boat launch and tent and trailer park. A rough car top canoe access is located along the northern shore via an access road that branches from Boundary Road (County Road 6). Boundary Road can be picked up from County Road 45 in the town of Sebright. Basic supplies are also available in Sebright.

Lake Definition

Elevation:	326 m (1,070 ft)
Mean Depth:	6 m (19.7 ft)
Max Depth:	7.3 m (24 ft)
Way Point:	44° 41' 00" Lat - N
	78° 11' 00" Lon - W

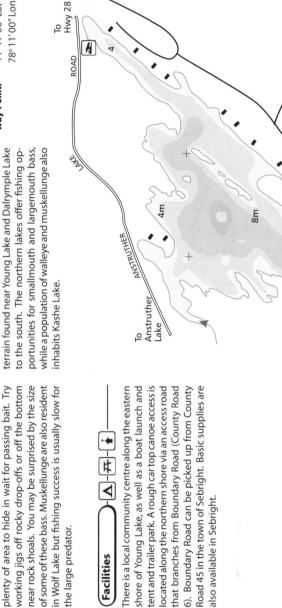

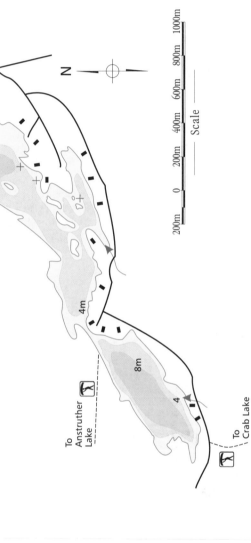

Kawarthas Key

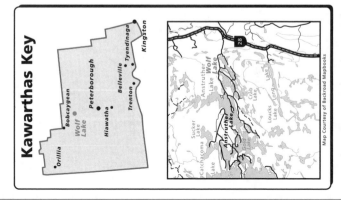

Wollaston Lake

Access

You can find Wollaston Lake near the village of Coe Hill east of Apsley. There are two direct routes to the lake. From the west, travel north along Highway 28 from Lakefield to Highway 620 at the town of Apsley. Head east along Highway 620 to Coe Hill. Look for the access road off the south side of Highway 620. If you cross over the Deer River, you have gone too far.

From the east, travel north along Highway 62 past the village of Gilmour to Highway 620. Take Highway 620 west over the Deer River to Coe Hill and to the access road off the south side of the county road. Follow the access road to the boat launch area on the north side of the lake.

Facilities

Along with the boat launch, there is tent and trailer park along the north side of the lake. For supplies, you can find a general store in the village of Coe Hill.

Fishing

Wollaston Lake is an active cottage destination lake with several camps and cottages found along the shoreline. Fishing pressure is consistent throughout the year and angling success remains fairly productive. The main fish species found in the lake are largemouth and smallmouth bass. Fishing for both species is fair for bass that range from 0.5-1.5 kg (1-3.5 lbs). Bass will hold near any sort of underwater or top water cover such as weeds or even boat docks. Another good area to locate bass is off the small island near the middle of the lake.

The two other main sport fish found in Wollaston Lake are lake trout and northern pike. Fishing for both fish is usually slow, although success for pike does pick up on occasion, especially during the spring. Look for pike along weed lines in the evening, especially in the weedier southwest arm of the lake. Trolling spoons, such as a Red Devil, or casting spinner baits can be productive.

There remains a very small natural population of lake trout in Wollaston Lake, although fishing success is limited to mainly the early portion of the season. Due to the fragile nature of the lake trout population; it is recommended to practise catch-and-release whenever possible. Special regulations have been enacted, such as slot sizes and winter fishing restrictions to help aid the trout population.

Other Options

If the fishing success is slow on Wollaston Lake, there are a number of nearby lakes in the area. In particular, **Sweets Lake** is found east of Wollaston Lake not far off the south side of County Road 620. The smaller lake offers angling opportunities for largemouth bass.

Lake Definition

Elevation:	244.7 m (803 ft)
Surface Area:	96.3 ha (238 ac)
Mean Depth:	13.5 m (44.5 ft)
Max Depth:	33.5 m (110 ft)
Perimeter:	15.5 km (9.6 mi)
Way Point:	45° 18' 00" Lat - N
	79° 47' 00" Lon - W

Kawarthas Key

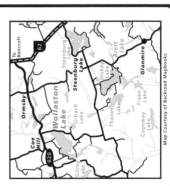

Map Courtesy of Backroad Mapbooks

Scale
200m 0 200m 400m 600m 800m 1000m

Young Lake

Access

This smaller Kawartha Lake is located north of Dalrymple Lake near the village of Sebright. To find the lake from the southwest, first follow Highway 12 to the town of Orillia. In the east end of Orillia, you can find County Road 44 off the north side of Highway 12. Take County Road 44 north approximately 4 km to County Road 45 (Monk Road). Follow County Road 45 east across County Road 169 and past the village of Sebright to the eastern shore of Young Lake. The lake is about 2 km north of Sebright.

Fishing

Angling success on Young Lake is surprisingly good despite the fact that the lake is easy to access and is fairly small. Fishing is best for largemouth and smallmouth bass, as bass can be found throughout the lake. Weed structure is the best place to look for holding bass; however, it is also possible to find the odd bass holding under shore structure such as cottage docks. You may be surprised when casting a spinner or jig past dock areas.

Walleye, northern pike and muskellunge also inhabit Young Lake. Fishing for walleye and northern pike is generally fair, while musky are usually much harder to find. Walleye average approximately 0.5-1 kg (1-2 lbs) in size, whereas pike and musky can be found in the 3 kg (6.5 lb) range. Some much larger pike and musky are caught and in Young Lake annually. Walleye and northern pike have similar habits throughout the summer months and if you are lucky you can catch a mix of the two. Look for these predators along weed lines; especially at dusk when they move in from the deeper portions of the lake looking for bait fish. There are also a number of significant shoal areas found around Young Lake that should be prime grounds for weed beds and hence bait fish activity. Look for weed growth in the 2-3 m (6.5-10 ft) range of shoals. These areas are usually prime feeding grounds in the evening or during overcast periods.

Facilities

There is a local community centre along the eastern shore of Young Lake, as well as a boat launch and tent and trailer park. A rough car top canoe access is located along the northern shore via an access road that branches from Boundary Road (County Road 6). Boundary Road can be picked up from County Road 45 in the town of Sebright. Basic supplies are also available in Sebright.

Other Options

At the town of Sebright, if yo[u] Road (County Road 6) north, you reach **Riley Lake** and **Kashe Lake**. [B]set amid rockier and rolling terrain tha[n] terrain found near Young Lake and Dalrym to the south. The northern lakes offer fishing [op]portunities for smallmouth and largemouth bass, while a population of walleye and muskellunge also inhabits Kashe Lake.

Lake Definition

Elevation:	226 m (741 ft)
Surface Area:	95.5 ha (235.8 ac)
Mean Depth:	4.8 m (16 ft)
Max Depth:	10.3 m (34 ft)
Perimeter:	3,900 m (12,795 ft)
Way Point:	44°43'00" Lat - N
	79°10'00" Lon - W

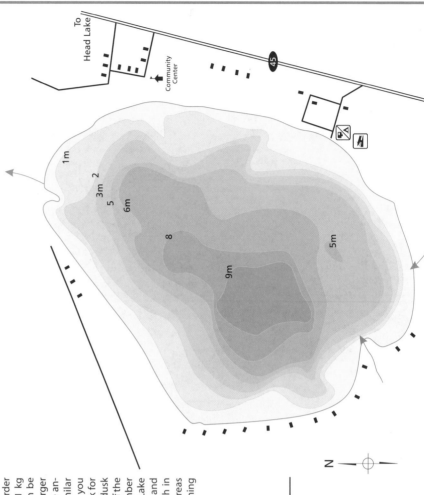

To Head Lake

To Sebright

Community Center

45

1m
2
3m
5
6m
8
9m
5m

N

Scale

100m 0 100m 200m 300m 400m 500m

Kawarthas Key

Young Lake
Orillia
Bobcaygeon
Peterborough
Hiawatha
Belleville
Trenton
Tyendinaga
Kingston

Young Lake
BOUNDARY Rd
Sebright
45
169
503

Map Courtesy of Backroad Mapbooks

Accommodations

Sales/Service

Tours/Guides

Backroad Mapbooks service providers directory is a list of services in the area covered in our books. They consist of Accomodiations, Sales/Services, and Tours/Guides. They are arranged alphabetically by City/Region, then by Business name. They flow from left to right.

SERVICE PROVIDERS DIRECTORY

To advertise your business in this section, call 1-877-520-5670 or 604-438-3474

King City

Fish Ontario

Live baits, Tackle, Licences.

Hwy 400 North
At Petro Canada Station
P.O. Box 38
King City, On, L78 1A4

Toll Free: 1-866-372-8013

P: 905-836-4566

Lakefield

Pine Vista

Four star quality & four seasons of fun. Situated 90 min NE of Toronto on spectacular Stoney Lake & featured in numerous fishing magazines. Units with kitchen, fireplace and deck with BBQ are great for group getaways. Stoney Lake's 1,100 islands offer excellent fishing for Pickerel, Bass, Muskie & Carp. Dock and Boat Rentals available.

Toll Free: 1-800-634-2848

P: 705-877-2108

www.pinevista.com

Alpine RV Resort & Cottage Rentals

Bright, spacious, 2 bedrooms complete with full kitchen, livingroom and 3 pc bathroom. Heated pool, brand new docks, boat rentals. Excellent fishing. Trails and tent sites available. Park backs onto hiking trail. Only 7 minutes away from downtown Lindsay.

46 Alpine Street.

Toll Free: 1-866-324-6447

www.alpinervresort.ca

Minden Live Bait & Tackle

Your highland headquarters for minnows, leeches, crayfish, and dew worms. Full line of Tackle, Accessories, Boating Licences, Abu Garcia Rods, Frenwick Rods, Tough Duck Clothing, Bear Spray, Shimano Rods & Reels, Hummingbird VHF Radios, Atlantis Underwater Cameras, Moccasins, Blue Jeans.

P: 705-286-4826

Hwy 35, Minden (across from Valuemart)

Rosedale Marina

A full service "Clean Marina" for all your boating needs. Licenced marine technicians servicing all makes and models. Transient and seasonal dockage, clean washrooms, showers, laundry facilities, boat accessories, bait, gasoline, diesel & pumpouts. Boat rentals and licences. Offer indoor/outdoor summer/winter storage.

P: 705-887-6921 F: 705-887-4433

52 Coldstream rd, Fenelon Falls

Three Castles Resort

Deluxe lakefront cottages and suites on Lower Buckhorn Lake in the town of Buckhorn. Fish for Bass, Muskie, Walleye, Perch, Blue Gill, etc. Short walk to town amenities, short paddle to Mississauga River, short drive to Petroglyph Provincial Park. Warsaw Caves, Peterborough.

Lock 31 of the Trent Severn Waterway

Toll Free: 1-800-924-2602

www.threecastles.com

ONTARIO'S URBAN FISHING PROGRAM

Virtually all of Ontario's larger urban centers are located on or near water and offer a fantastic diversity of doorstep angling opportunities. In 2004, the Ministry of Natural Resources initiated a three-year pilot program in southern Ontario to improve angling opportunities in and around urban centres and increase participation in angling by urban residents, particularly youth.

The urban fishing program involves improving access to fishing sites, installing fish attractor structures, organizing fishing derbies and festivals, publishing infomation on where to fish (and for what) and providing loaner fishing equipment.

So get fishing! For more information on urban fishing opportunities in your area contact your local MNR office.

Notes

mile Lake.
sam Lake,
Belmont Lake.
- Bald Lake.

Drown Your Campfire!

Be Careful with Fire!

 Ontario

Lake Index

The Author

Jason Marleau was born in Sudbury, Ontario. While growing up in Central Ontario, he had the opportunity to experience and enjoy Ontario's great outdoors. After graduating from the University of Ottawa, Jason spent a few years exploring British Columbia, where he met Russell and Wesley Mussio from Backroad Mapbooks.

This monumental meeting not only changed the career path of Jason but has also benefited many outdoor enthusiasts in Ontario and across the country. Jason has authored or co-authored over a dozen **Backroad Mapbooks** and **Fishing Mapbook** titles.

Despite his growing family commitments (we are proud to welcome River J to our family), Jason continues to be an avid outdoorsmen. Whenever he is not working on guidebooks, he is enjoying the great outdoors.

IMPORTANT PHONE NUMBERS

Ministry of Natural Resources
General Inquiry .... (800) 667-1940 (Bilingual)
.... mnr.nric@mnr.gov.on.ca

Outdoors Card (Licenses, Customer Service) .... (800) 387-7011

Aurora, Greater Toronto Area .... (905) 713-7400

Minden .... (705) 286-1521

Peterborough .... (705) 755-2001

Tweed .... (613) 478-2330

Parks
Reservations .... (888) ONT-PARK
.... www.ontarioparks.com

Balsam Lake .... (705) 454-3324

Silent Lake .... (613) 339-2807

Emily .... (705) 799-5170

Crime Stoppers (Poaching) .... (800) 222-TIPS (8477)

Invading Species Hotline .... (800) 563-7711

Sport Fish Contaminant Monitoring Programme .... (800) 820-2716

Updates .... www.backroadmapbooks.com

Tourism, Resorts & Lodges
Ontario Tourism .... (800) ONT-ARIO
Resorts Ontario .... (705) 325-9115

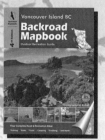

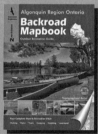